J. O'Beirne Crowe

The Amra Choluim Chilli of Dallan Forgaill

Now Printed for the First Time from the Original Irish in Lebor

J. O'Beirne Crowe

The Amra Choluim Chilli of Dallan Forgaill
Now Printed for the First Time from the Original Irish in Lebor

ISBN/EAN: 9783337121037

Printed in Europe, USA, Canada, Australia, Japan

Cover: Foto ©ninafisch / pixelio.de

More available books at **www.hansebooks.com**

THE

AMRA CHOLUIM CHILLI

OF

DALLAN FORGAILL:

NOW PRINTED FOR THE FIRST TIME FROM THE ORIGINAL IRISH

IN

Lebor na huiore,

A MS. IN THE LIBRARY OF THE ROYAL IRISH ACADEMY;

WITH

A LITERAL TRANSLATION AND NOTES,
A GRAMMATICAL ANALYSIS OF THE TEXT,
AND COPIOUS INDEXES.

BY

J. O'BEIRNE CROWE, A.B.;

GOLD MEDALLIST IN ANCIENT CLASSICS AND ANCIENT LITERATURE;
GOLD MEDALLIST IN THE CELTIC LANGUAGES AND LITERATURE;
LATE PROFESSOR OF CELTIC, QUEEN'S COLLEGE, GALWAY;
AND EXAMINER IN CELTIC FOR THE QUEEN'S UNIVERSITY
IN IRELAND.

DUBLIN:

McGLASHAN AND GILL, 50, UPPER SACKVILLE-STREET.
LONDON: WILLIAMS & NORGATE, 14, HENRIETTA-ST., COVENT GARDEN;
AND 20, SOUTH FREDERICK-STREET, EDINBURGH.

1871.

THE EDITOR'S INTRODUCTION.

T HE occasion of the composition of the Amra, or Elegy
of Columb Cille, is fully stated in the ancient preface ;
it is therefore unnecessary to repeat what is there already
given. In order, however, that the reader may be able
to carry with him from the outset a fair idea of both
Author and Poem, I shall here quote a few passages from
Colgan's Life of St. Dallan (Acta Sanctorum, p. 203, *et
seqq.*).

"In the times of Aed,[1] son of Ainmere, monarch of
Ireland, about the year of Christ 580,[2] there flourished in
the same kingdom a man of illustrious ancestry, by name
Eochaid, and by cognomen Dallan, who splendidly adorned
nobility of race by great comeliness of virtues. He
was born in a district of Connacht bordering on Ulster,

The following notes are Colgan's own :
anything I add will be enclosed in
brackets, and marked " ED." Colgan in-
troduces his notes with the remark, " Because the acts of this saint have not come
to my hands, these things which have
presented themselves about him as worthy
of remark, I have taken chiefly from the
history of the Acts of the Synod of Druimm
Ceta, and from the Life of St. Columb."

[1] *In the times of Aed, Monarch of Ireland.* So is expressly held in the Preface
to the Acts of the aforesaid synod of
Druimm Ceta, and in the Life of St.
Columb, cap. 218.

[2] *About the Year of Christ,* 580. King
Aed, according to the common catalogue
of the kings of Ireland, and the Annals of
Donnegall [Four Masters], began to reign
in the year 571, or, according to others,
576, and he reigned 27 years. With his
time then, and so in the year 580, St.
Dallan flourished, especially since he lived
after the death of St. Columb, who died,
according to Ussher, in the year 597, or
at least after the year 590. [The year
597 is the true date. See Dr. Reeves's
Introduction to his Adamnan's St. Columba, p. lxxviii].—ED.

which the ancients called *Masrige*, and *Cathrige Sleacht*,[3] but which the moderns name *Teallach Eathuch*.

His mother's name was Forchella,[4] from whom himself, too, it is thought, is called Dallan Forgaill,[5] or Forcellius ; and his father was Colla,[6] son of Erc, of the race of Colla surnamed Uais,[7] King of Ireland ; his cousin-german was Maidoc of Ferns,[8] the very renowned archbishop of Leinster, grandson of the same Erc from his son Sedna, or Sedonius.[9]

Colgan, after speaking of the great learning of Eochaid, and explaining the word *Dallan* (the blind), an epithet which he received from his having, through the severity of his studies, lost the use of his eyes, thus proceeds :—

" He wrote in the native speech and in ancient style several little works, which cannot in later ages be easily penetrated by many otherwise well-versed in the old native idiom and antiquity; and hence they are illustrated by our more learned antiquaries with scattered commentaries, and as rare monuments of our ancient language and antiquity, it is customary to lecture on them, and expound them in the schools of antiquaries of our nation.

" Among these is one panegyric or poem, now and

---

[3] *Masrige, &c.* Thus it is held in the aforesaid Preface.

[4] *His mother's name was Forchella.* Thus is it held in the same place, and is it gathered from Blessed Marianus Gormanus, and from the author of the Martyrology of Tamlacht, who calls him the son of *Forgall*. But his father was not called Forgall or Forchella, but Colla, . . . whence that was his mother's name.

[5] *From whom himself, it is thought, is called Forgaill, or Forchellius.* So the same Preface testifies.

[6] *But his father was Colla, son of Erc.* So the same Preface, and the Life of St. Columb, cap. 2, 18, and the Genealogical Monologium, cap. 12.

[7] *Son of Erc, of the race of Colla Uais.* Thus it is held in the same place, but the Genealogical Monologium says that this Erc was, from his son Feredach, grandson of King Colla. But the Life of St. Maedoc, and others, say that the same Erc was the grandfather of both St. Dallan and St. Maedoc; but the grandfather of St. Maedoc was not the grandson of King Colla, but many degrees removed from him. . . . And this opinion pleases me the more, because it is more likely that those who lived at the same time were the same distance of degrees from the common trunk, than that one of them should be many more.

[8] [Here Colgan refers to his Life of Maedoc, whose day is the 31st January].—ED.

[9] *Grandson of the same Erc from his son Sedna.* So the Irish Life of St. Maedoc, chapter 72, &c.

always held in great esteem, on the praises of St. Columb, and entitled *Amra Choluim Chille*,[10] that is, " The Praises of Columb of the Churches." The occasion of the composition of this little work is recorded to be as follows : After St. Columb had come from Britain to Ireland to settle certain disputes which had arisen between the monarch of Ireland, Aed, his relative, and the chiefs of Dal Riata and Leinster, and other subjects ; and after he had attended before the same king, and the nobles of the kingdom, in a certain synod of Druimm Ceta, assembled for this purpose in the region of Cianachta,[11] while the assembly was being broken up, and all things were succeeding according to the wishes of St. Columba, with the hope of general peace and concord, St. Dallan comes to St. Columb, and offers him a certain poem, which he had composed in his praise. But while that poem was being partly read, and the holy man was strongly feeling certain sudden emotions of vain complacency, he was admonished by St. Baithene, his disciple, then standing near, that a great troop of evil demons appeared scoffing above his head, and when the holy man with astonishment saw the troop, he was struck with compunction of heart, and immediately he forbids the praises written by St. Dallan to be further produced or published : adding that no one [should be praised] in life, which he might badly end ; that he alone who had run well in the *stadium*, and had ended his race successfully, should be praised after his death. And when Dallan could by no

---

[10] *Amra Cho'uim Chil'e*, that is, *the Praises of Columb of the Churches*. I have in my possession one copy of this work, beautifully written, but, putting aside a few scattered commentaries which it contains, it is penetrable to a few only to-day, and these most learned. [I shall try to make the present translation rank me as one of the successors, though *longo intervallo*, of Colgan's "*peritissimi*."]—Ed.

[11] *In the region of Cianachta.* Druimm Ceta is a place in the Diocese and County of Derry, at the River Roe, to-day and always venerable especially on account of the many pilgrimages, and the public Theophory which, on the festival of All Saints, in memory of the aforesaid synod there celebrated, is there annually made, with an immense concourse from all the neighbouring districts.

contrivance obtain the publication of the praises he had written, he insisted that he might be allowed to follow out his [St. Columb's] life, in case that it should be happily ended, with praises after his death : and this he accordingly obtained.

"The Saint accordingly, having returned to Britain, died after some years, and immediately as soon as he died, St. Dallan received by angelic ministry the announcement of his death, and composed that very learned little work which we have mentioned: and when he had finished this, he was regifted with the[12] immediately-lost light of his eyes, and further received a promise that the person, who would recite these praises from memory and from mind, would close his life with a happy end." Of the other works of Dallan, Colgan says :—

"He composed, also, another poem[13] for the death and funeral praise of Senan, Bishop of Inis Cathaig (Scattery Island), which, on account of antiqueness of style and antique gracefulness, is among those fond of antiquity always in great esteem : and on account of the grace of preservation from blindness and other special indulgences, which are believed to be granted by God to him who recites it from memory, it is among devout persons held in great veneration.

He composed also a third little work in praise of St. Conall,[14] surnamed Coel, Abbat of Inis Coel,[15] in Tir Connail (now Iniskeel in Donegall). Of him also he

---

[12] [The meaning is that Dallan, to whom Columba allowed the use of his eyes while making the poem, lost that use immediately on finishing it, but was immediately regifted with it].—ED.

[13] *Also another poem.* I have in my possession this little work, which can hardly be taken in to-day without illustrations of antiquaries. [There is a copy of this Amra in H. 2. 16 : T. C. D.: and another in II. 3. 17: T. C. D., and fragments in various manuscripts].—ED.

[14] *In praise of St. Conall.* This is recorded in the aforesaid Preface, but whether it is still extant or not is unknown to me.

[15] *Conall, Abbatt of Inis Coel.* This church is in an island, surrounded by the

begged strenuously that, by the intervention of his prayers and merits, he might deserve to enjoy the honour of a tomb the same with himself (that is, to be buried with him), and this, granted by the Divine goodness, he obtained."

The above extracts, regarding Dallan and his poetry, will be quite sufficient. I shall now proceed to give my reader the plan of publication I intend to adopt.

The work will be finished in two Parts. Part I. (the present) contains the Ancient Preface; the *Exordium*, or Prelude to the Amra and the Amra proper with their ancient commentaries, and a literal translation of the whole. Part II. will contain topographical, biographical, and historical notes; a critical and grammatical analysis of every word in the text, and copious Indexes. And as the Lebor Brec's[16] Preface to the Amra supplies several important records omitted in that of Lebor na hUidre, this preface also will be given, together with the marginal notes and secondary glosses of the present copy, and with literal translations. The poetic characteristics of our poem will be examined in an Appendix, which will also say a word or two on Irish poetry in general. The text, to distinguish it from the commentaries, is given in large letters, and exactly as it stands in the original, and on the whole I have strong hopes that my Amra, when completed, will receive the approbation of my spiritual friends, St. Columb and St. Dallan above, as well as that of my literary friends here below.

DUBLIN, *August*, 1871.   J. O'B. C.

---

ocean, in the district of Tirconnaill, which is called *Bugellaigh*, and in the diocese of Raphoe, and in this church St. Conall is venerated on the 12th May. [St. Dallan's day is the 29th January].—ED.

[16] A defect of one page in Lebor na hUidre is supplied from the Lebor Brec, which, though only a fragment, fortunately preserves the last leaf of the Amra, and the greater portion of the preface.]—Ed.

Loc do'no ꝑem[ḟ]ocul-ꞃa ceꞇuꞃ Dꞃuimm Ceꞇa, aꞃ iꞅ
ann doꞃonad in móꞃ-dáil Dꞃomma Ceꞇa : in alio locó
immoꞃo, doꞃonad coꞃꝑ ino immuin o ꝼein immaċ, uꞇ poꞃꞇ
apꝑaꞃeꞇ. In amꞃíꞃ Aedae meic Anmeꞃeċ doꞃigned :
peꞃꞃo—Dallán Foꞃgaill do Maꞃꞃaigib Maige Sleċꞇ :
ꞇucaiꞇ—aꞃ ꞃoċꞇain ꞃíċhio dó ꝼéin, ⁊ alíꞅ ꞃeꞃ ꞃe. Tꞃí
ꞇucaiꞇe ueꞃo aꞃ a ꞇanic Colum Cille a hAlbain in
hEꞃino in ꞇan ꞅin .i. do ꝼúaꞃlucud Scannlán Móiꞃ, meic
Cinn Fáelad, ꞃíg Oꞃꞃaiꞃe, ꝼꞃiꞅ in deoċaid iꞃ ꞃáꞇaiꞃeꞅ,
⁊ do aꞃꞇud inna ꝼiled in hEꞃind (aꞃ ꞃobaꞃ ino innaꞃba
aꞃ a ꞇꞃomdaċꞇ, aꞃ nobio .xxx. i cléiꞃ cac olloman, ⁊
axu. i cléiꞃ caċ anꞃaid) : ⁊ do ꞃioꞇgud eꞇeꞃ ꝼiꞃu
hEꞃenn, ⁊ Alban im Dal Ríaꞇa. ⁊ iꞅ ed aꞇbeꞃaꞇ no con
acca Colum Cille Eꞃinn in ꞇan ꞅin, aꞃ nobid bꞃéiꞇ daꞃ
a ꞃuilib : ⁊ iꞅ ed ꝼoꞇeꞃa ꞅein, aꞃ ꞃogell ꞃemi ꞃein ic
dul ꞇaꞃiꞅ na ꝼégbad Eꞃind o ꝼein immaċ, diceꞅ :

      Fil ꞃuiln glaiꞅ,
     Fégbaꞃ Éꞃinn daꞃ a haiꞃ :
    No con ácebá íaꞃmoꞇhá
    Fiꞃu Eꞃend náċ a mmna.

Coꞇudċaid iaꞃam Colum Cille iꞅ inn aiꞃeċꞇ ocuꞅ
coꞃéꞃꞃaċꞇ ꞃocaide ꞃemi do ꝼáelꞇi ꝼꞃiꞅ. Mad iaꞃ
ꞃonċaꞃ ele, immoꞃo, ní eꞃꞃaċꞇ neċ ꞃemi aċꞇ Dommnall
mac in ꞃíg, aꞃ aꞇꞃubaiꞃꞇ in ꞃí co ná heiꞃꞃed neċ ꞃemi :
aꞃ ꞃoꞃiꞇiꞃ aní imm o ꞇánc, ⁊ ní ꞃ'ba maiꞇ leiꞃ a
ꞇiċꞇain, aꞃ ní n'bo áil leiꞃ aꞃꞇud na ꝼiled, no ꞇuaꞃlucud

FORESPEECH.

THE place for this forespeech, firstly, is Druimm Ceta, for it is in it was made the great meeting of Druimm Ceta: in a different place, however, was made the body of the hymn from that forth, as appears after. In the time of Aed, son of Anmere, it was made: author—Dallan Forgaill of the Masraige of Mag Slecht: cause—for reaching of heaven for himself and for others through it. Now there are three causes for which Colum Cille came from Alba to Eriu that time—namely, for the releasing of Scanlann Mór, son of Cend Faelad, king of the Osrarians, with whom he went in pledgeship: and for the staying of the poets in Eriu (for they were in banishment on account of their burdensomeness, for there used to be thirty in the company of each *Ollom*, and fifteen in the company of each *Anrad*): and for pacification between the men of Eriu and of Alba about Dal Riata. And it is it they say, that Colum Cille by no means saw Eriu that time, for there used to be a bandage over his eyes; and it is it that caused that, because he promised before that at going past it, that he would not view Eriu from that forth, saying :—

> There is a grey eye
> That will view Eriu backwards :
> By no means will it see afterwards
> The men of Eriu or its women.

Colum Cille then came to the assembly, and several rose up before him for welcome to him. If it is according to another tradition, however, there rose not up one before him but Domnall, the king's son, for the king said that there should not rise up one before him; for he knew that about which he had come, and his coming was not thought

Scannlaín. Conid and ṡein ṗobennaċ Colum Cille inni Domnall, aṗ ṗobo aiṗmeta connici ṡein. Ꝝo ṗ'bu olc laṗ in ṗíꝥain a bennachad, aṗ ṗobo leṡ-mac di é : ꝥo ṗoṡeṗꝥaiꝥ in clépeċ ṡṗia, con éṗbaiṗt-ṡi ṡṗiṡ in clépeċ : " Ꝛomóṗ in ċoṗṗaiꝥeċt ṗoṗ a tái." " Iṡ cet duitṡiu," aṗ in clépeċ, "bíṫ ṗoṗ coṗṗaiꝥeċt ṗoṗ a tái : iṡ cet duitṡiu," aṗ in clépeċ, "bíṫ ṗoṗ coṗṗaiꝥeċt." Conid and ṡein ṗoṗoad-ṡi i cuiṗṗ, co ṗaꝥaib a hinailt ṗoṗ aċiṗiuꝥud in clépiꝥ, co ṗoṗaid ṡide hi cuiṗṗ ele : co ṗilet na dá ċuiṗṗ ṡin o ṡein ille in Druim Cheta, ut alii dicunt.

Táncataṗ íaṗ ṡein na ṗilid iṡ inn aiṗeċt ꝛ dúan molta léo dó ꝛ aiodbṡi ainm in chíúil ṡin ; ocuṡ ba céol deṗṡ-caiꝥteċ hé, ut Colmán mac Lénéne diꝛit :

Luin oc heolaib, uinꝥi o[c] diṗnaib,
Cṗota bann áeteċ oc cṗothaib ṗíꝥna,
Ꝛíꝥ ic Domnall, doṗd ic aiodbṡi,
Adand oc ɕainmill, colc oc mo choilc-ṡe.

ꝛ in óen[ṗ]eċt doꝥnítíṗ in ceól ṡin. Cotáṁic míad men-man do'n ċleṗeoch, co ṗ'bo lán int áeṗ húaṡ a chind ó demnaib, co ṗoṗailṗiꝥed do báiċin ṡein, ꝛ co ṗochaiṗiꝥ ṡide in clépeċ, ꝛ co tuc in clépeċ íaṗ ṡein a chend ṗo choim, ꝛ con deṗna aċṗiꝥe, ꝛ co túaṗꝥaib iaṗ ṡein a chend aṗ a choim, ꝛ co ṗóemid ceo móṗ di a chind, ꝛ co ṗoṗcáilit aṗ na demna ṗiaṡ in céo ṡin. Da cét déc dan lín na ṗiled, ut diꝛit quidam :—

Ṗeċt do Mael Choba na clíaṗ
Ic hIbuṗ chind Tṗáċta ċíaṗ,
Da cét déc ṗiled ṗoṗṗúaiṗ
Ꝛeṡ inn Ibaṗ aníaṗ-thúaid.
Coinnmed teóṗam blíadann bind
Doṗat dóib Máel Coba in cinꝥ :
Méṗaid co lá bṗácha báin
Do chenéol delbda Demáin.

well of by him, for the staying of the poets, or the releasing of Scannlan was not pleasing to him. So that it is then Columb Cille blessed this Domnall, because he was reverent to that extent. So that his blessing was thought ill of by the queen, for he was a stepson to her : so that the cleric grew angry towards her, so that she said to the cleric : " Very great is the craneing on which thou art." " Thou hast leave," says the cleric, " to be on a craneing on which thou art : thou hast leave," says the cleric, " to be on a craneing." So that it is then she was turned into a crane, so that her handmaid took to reproaching the cleric, so that she turned into another crane : so that those two cranes are from that hither in Druim Ceta, as some say.

The poets after that came into the assembly, and a poem of praising with them for him, and *aidbsi* (chorus) is the name of that music ; and a surpassing music was it, as Colman Mac Lenene said :—

Blackbirds beside swans, ounces beside masses,
Forms of peasant women beside forms of queens,
Kings beside Domnall, a murmur beside a chorus,
A taper beside a candle [is] a sword beside my sword.

And together they used to make that music. Dignity of mind came for the cleric, so that the sky above his head was full from demons, so that this was manifested to Baithene ; and that he rebuked the cleric, and that the cleric after that brought his head under cover, and that he did penance, and that he raised after that his head from its cover, and that a great fog sprang from his head, and that the demons scattered from it before that fog. And twelve hundred was the number of the poets as a certain one said :—

As Mael Choba of the companies was once
At Ibar Chind Trachta in the west :
Twelve hundred poets—he them found
By the Yew in the north-west,
Refection of three melodious years
Mael Coba the chief gave to them :
It shall live to the day of pale judgment
For the well-formed race of Deman.

Co popopt Colum Cille iap pein na pileou ⁊ con epbaipt
ppi hAeo :

> Copmac cain buic neoic,
> Nua molca, cpína peoic :
> Ip eo polezup poc-cpaeo—
> Ceinmaip molciap, maipg áepciap, Aʼeo!
> Cáin in púg ap a paep-[p]aigcib pugchiap ;
> Maipg in iac ecnaipc aipciap !
> Apao cloc : cáin in péim piaoaic bí :
> Oopúapcec máini molcaioi.

Oopónao coinomeo na pileo iap pein po Eʼpino ⁊
pooígbaic iap pein a clíapa .i. xxiiii. i cléip ino Olloman
⁊ xii. i cléip ino ánpaio.

Ip iap pin bái Colum Cille i cuincio Scanoláin pop
Aeo, ⁊ ni capoao oó ; con epbaipt pium oan ppi Aeo, ip
é nonzébao a appa imme imm iapmepgi ce bé bale nobec,
⁊ pocomallao amlaio. Colmán macc Comzelláin, immopo,
ip é puc inm bpeic ecep pipu Epeno ⁊ Alban, ⁊ oo Oál
Ríaca oo pioe ; ⁊ ip pír oopigni Colum Cille inm báioe
in can popo lenam béc in Colmán, uc oixic :

> A chubup con : a anim glan ;
> Apo poíc ouic : oale poíc oam.

⁊ apbepc Culum Cille ip é oogénao rícuguo ecep
pipu Epeno ⁊ Alban : ⁊ ip i bpec puc, "a pecc
⁊ a plógeo la pipu Epeno oogpér," ap ip [r]lógeo la
ponnaib oogpér : "a cain ⁊ a cobac la pipu Alban ;" no,
"am muip-coblac nammá la pipu Alban : ó pein immac,
immopo, la pipu hEpenn."

Tánic iapam Oallan, apo-ollom hEpenn in can pin
oo acallaim Cholu[i]m Chilli, conio ano pogab in pem-
pocul oó : ⁊ ni peléic Colum Cille oó a oénam pec a-
pein, con oepnao in ampip a éipcecca, ap apbepc ppi

So that Columb Cille after that stayed the poets, and that he said to Aed :—

Cormac well broke battle,
New [his] praisings, withered [his] jewels :
It is it I have read wheel-poetry—
A blessing that one is praised, woe that one is satirized,
    Aed !
Fair the juice which from its free lawns is sucked :
Woe the absent land that is satirized !
Renowned ladder : fair the course they living drive ;
The treasures of praisers remain.

The refection of the poets was after that made over Eriu, and their companies were diminished after that—namely [only] twenty-four in the company of the Ollom, and twelve in the company of the Anrad.

It is after that Columb Cille was making the demand of Scandlan upon Aed, and he was not given to him ; so that he said accordingly to Aed, that it is he [Scandlan] who would get his shoes about him [Columb] about midnight, whatever place he should be, and it was so fulfilled. Now, Colman, son of Comgellan, it is he who gave the judgment between the men of Eriu and of Alba, and he was of Dal Riata ; and it is with him Columb Cille made the embrace the time the Colman was a little infant, as he said :—

O tree of hounds : O pure soul !
This is a kiss to thee ; deal thou a kiss to me.

And Columb Cille said, it is he who would make pacification between the men of Eriu and of Alba : and it is the judgment he gave, " Their expedition and their hosting with the men of Eriu always," for there is hosting with territories always : " their tribute and their exaction with the men of Alba ;" or, " their sea-gathering only with the men of Alba, but from that forth with the men of Eriu."

Then Dallan, chief Ollom of Eriu that time, came to converse with Columb Cille, so that it is then he recited the forespeech for him : and Columb Cille did not allow him the making of it beyond that, that he should make it

maṗb baṗ chubaid : ⁊ iṗ do ċenonaib poṫṗíall Dallán
a díain do ḋénam. Doṗaiṗnġeṗc cṗá Colum Cille do
Dallán inmaṗṗa ⁊ coṗċc in calman aṗ in molad-ṗa,
⁊ ní ṗaġaib, acc nem dó ḟéin ⁊ do ceċ oén non-
ġebad caċ día, ⁊ dopucébad eceṗ chéill ⁊ ḟoġuṗ,
uc quidam diṗic :—

Ampa Coluim—caċ día
Cep é nodġeba co pollan,
Roṗía in ḟind-[ḟ]laiċ ḟia,
Roíṗ Dia do Dallán.

Cṗí comaṗca, immoṗo, doṗac Colum Cille dó in can
doġénad .i. maṗcaċ eiċ alaid noinniṗṗed dó écṗecc
Coluim Chilli, ⁊ in cécna ḟoccul noṗáidṗed in maṗcaċ
commad hé coṗaċ in molca, .⁊ a ṗuile do lécuo dó céin
nobeċ ic a ḋénam. Ic Aċ Féne dan im Mide doṗonad
in molad-ṗa, uc Mael Suċain diṗic: aoféc, immoṗo,
Ḟendomnach, comaṗba Colu[i]m Chilli, iṗ íaṗ Sliġe
Aṗṗail ṗocanad, ó cá Dún nan Aiṗbed coṗ in cṗoiṗ ic
Ciġ Lommá[i]n. Anamain eceṗ dá nin inṗo .i. nin i
coṗṗuċ in molcai ⁊ nin in a deṗiud .i. "Ni diṗ [ṗ]céoil"
⁊ "Nimúain." No iṗ ġobul di .i. ṗecne de-chubaid .i.
dá ṗon no a cṗí do cinnṗcecul o aén ḟid beoṗ .i. diaid
indiaid, ⁊ ṗon o ḟid iṗ écṗamail in a díad ṗide.

Dia, Dia, ⁊c. Iṗ aiṗi emnaṗ in céc ḟocal aṗ abela,
no aṗ lainni in molca, uc eṗc, Deuṗ, Deuṗ meuṗ, ⁊c.
Iṗ é, immoṗo, a ainm ṗein laṗ in Ġoedel "aceṗṗuċ
in ġuċn ġnáċ," aṗ bíci cṗi quale coṗmaile labaṗcha ic
ḟiledaib na Ġoedeilġe .i. aaceṗṗuċ in ġuċn ġláč, ⁊
ainṗi-mod, ⁊ adíabul, ⁊ iṗ í ṗo aiċne ceċai díb. Iṗ é
inc aiċeṗṗuċ quidem emnad óen-ḟocuil in oen-iniud iṗ ind
ṗunn ⁊ cen lenamain dé ó ṗein immaċ. Iṗ é, immoṗo,
ainṗe-mod a inniṗein o mud inund .i. inc óen-ḟocul do ṗád

in the time of his death ; for he said, to one dead it was fitting : and it is of headlets [*capitula*] Dallan proceeded to make his poem. Now Columb Cille promised to Dallan the gifts and products of the earth for this praising, and he did not take them, but heaven for himself and for every one who would recite it each day, and would understand it between sense and sound, as a certain one said:

> Columb's Amra—every day
> Whoever will recite it completely,
> Will reach the good bright kingdom
> Which God granted to Dallan.

Now three signs Columb Cille gave him the time he should make it—namely, a rider of a speckled steed would announce to him the death of Columb Cille, and the first word the rider would utter, that it was to be the beginning of the praising, and that his eyes would be allowed to him, while he should be at the making of it. At Feni's Ford again in Mide [Meath] this praising was made, as Mael Suthain said : Ferdomnach, however, successor of Columb Cille, declares it is behind Assal's Way it was chanted, from where the Fort of the Balustrades is to the Cross at Lomman's House. *Anamain* between two *Ashes* this ; that is, *Ash* in the beginning of the praising, and *Ash* in its ending ; namely, *Ni dis* [*s*]*ceoil* and *Nimuain*. Or it is *fork of two*, that is, bi-rhyming narration ; that is, to begin two sounds or three from one tree still ; that is, one after another; and a sound from a tree which is different after that.

" God, God," &c. It is why he doubles the first word— on account of the rapidity and avidity of the praising, as is, *Deus, Deus meus*, &c. But the name of that with the Goedel is "return to a usual sound ;" for there be three similar standards of expression with the poets of the Goedel; that is, *re-return to a usual sound*, and *renarration mode*, and *reduplication*, and this is the mark of each of them. The "return," indeed, is a doubling of one word in one place in the round, without adhering to it from that forth. The "renarration mode," again, is renarrating from a like mode ; that is, the one word—to say it frequently in the

commenıc ıp ınꝺ punꝺ con ecapcaıꝺecc pocul ele
ecappu, uc epc hoc .ı.

> Rıc ın pıcbe pıclap maʒ,
> Rıc ın ꝺam cpí coécaıc ʒlonꝺ :
> Rıc ın ʒılla ʒupmap, ʒanꝺ,
> Popacaıb Cú Ꝺınıpc ꝺonn.

Ir é, ımmopo, aꝺfabul .ı. apıllıuꝺ .ı. ꝺo-emnaꝺ, uc
epc hoc, .ı.

> Aʒup, áʒup, ıap cém céın,
> bıc ı péın peın, ní píc pıc :
> Amal các các, co bpác bpác,
> In cec cpác cpác, cıꝺ pcíc pcíc.

Ꝺa epnaıl ꝺíb po ır ınꝺ pempocul-po—aceppuc ın
ʒucn ʒnác, ocup aınnpı-moꝺ : aınpe-moꝺ, ımmopo, nammá
poʒabap ı cupp ınꝺ ımmuın.

ꝺᓮa, ꝺᓮa—ꝺORRoʒus ᚱᓮa cᓮas ᓮNN a
ʒNᑌ'ᓮs .ı. acaʒup Ꝺıa, no ʒuꝺım Ꝺıa, píapıu chíap ın
a ʒnúıp, no ın can, no ınꝺ ınꝺbaıꝺ cíap.

cᑌʟᑌ cᚱᓮa Neᓮc.—Popcceꝺ, no popmolaꝺ pıl
híc : ⁊ con na bıcíp ʒnee popcceꝺa, poıp ın ꝺıcneꝺ ⁊,
ꝺocneꝺ ⁊ cennacpop, uc quıꝺam ꝺıcunc. bıꝺ ꝺan néıc .ı.
ʒuın, uc ꝺıcıcup :—

> Rob é ꝺo lecc ı papce
> Iap ꝺo néıc péol pıpaıcce :
> Ruccap ı capp ınꝺıaıꝺ pıll
> Ꝺo [P]pacc, a pcáıl, ꝺı á coem-chıll.

.ı. Amal céıc cappac pepꝺa cpé cac, co pop amlaıꝺ
ꝺec m' anım-pea cpía cacn [ꝺ]emna ꝺocum nıme.

cᑌʟᑌ .ı. popcceꝺ punꝺ ınconꝺılıꝺ, ap ır "cul" ın pocul
ʒnácac, acc pocuıll ın pılí .u. punꝺ ꝺo línaꝺ na
pılıꝺecca ; no, ꝺo búaıcnıʒuꝺ na pocul cpía ꝺíʒbaıl ocup
cpıa córpmach ocup cpía ıncumpʒuʒuꝺ ꝺo ꝺénam ıncıb.
⁊ acác cpí ʒnee paıp .ı. ꝺıcneꝺ ⁊ ꝺocneꝺ ocup cennacpop.

round, with an intervention of other words between them, as is this :

> Came the foam [which] the plain filters,
>> Came the ox through fifty warriors ;
> [So] came the keen, active lad,
>> [Whom] brown Cu Dinisc left.

But "reduplication" is, namely, "refolding;" that is, "bi-geminating," as is this :

> I ask, I ask, after long, long,
>> To be in pain, pain, not peace, peace :
> Like each, each, till judgment, judgment,
>> In each time, time, though fatigue, fatigue.

Two divisions of these in this forespeech : "return to a usual sound," and "renarration-mode ;" but "renarration-mode" only in the body of the hymn.

GOD, GOD—I HAVE ASKED HIM ERE I COME TO HIS FACE. .ı. I implore of God, or I ask of God ere I come to his face, or the time, or the period I come.

FOR CHARIOTS THROUGH BATTLE.—"Obscuration," or "superabundance," here ; and that appearances of "obscuration" might not exist, the "be-heading," and "bi-heading," and "head-changing" have been established, as some persons say. "Neit" also means, that is, *wound*, as is said :

> May thy monument at dawn-breeze be
> After thy death-wound a sail ever to be driven ;
> Borne may [she] be in a chariot after a horse
> Thy wife, O hero, to her beautiful church.

That is : as a serrated chariot goes through battle, may it be so my soul shall go through the battle of demons to heaven.

"Obscuration" here in a special way, for *cul* is the usual word ; but the poet added .*u.* here for filling of the poetry ; or for making the words hard to be known through diminution and through increase and through immutation being made in them. And there are three forms on it, [on "obscuration,"] that is, "be-heading," and "bi-heading," and "head-changing." The "be-heading" is—to cut its own head

Iſ é in oiċneo a chenn oo ʒaiṫ oo'no [ḟ]ocul ⁊ cen ní
ele in a inao, uṫ oixiṫ poeṫa :—

> Oál poṫáluſ—móſ in baeſ—
> Iſ ino aſuſ huaſ Oſuimm :
> A mmo Chomoiu, a ſí ſú ſá,
> bui biu ba béſ ni ṫíaſ.

" Rú ſá"—iſ é in oeſmeſeċṫ ano ſein : aſ iſ "ſún ſán"
ſooleċṫ. Iſ e, ueſo, m ooċneo oa ceno ſaiſ .i. a ċenn
ſém ⁊ ceno ele ; ⁊ commao é a oſleſ in liṫṫiſ oé-
oenaċ ino [ḟ]ocuil oo emnao, amal ooʒneṫea "benn"
oo'noí aſ "ben," uṫ oiciṫuſ :—

> Lainn ſiſ néiṫ ſaoḃ coſcſa ;
> Téiṫ oáiʒ Oe oemin ni ṫeſcoa ;
> Foſſuim ṫeno oo ċſuno oċṫʒa ;
> Ʒnaċ cenn i cſúḃ Chon eċṫʒa.

Commao hi ſéṫ nobéṫ in oeſmeſeċṫ híc .i. a chenn ſéin
ſoſ ino [ḟ]iſ úṫ ⁊ cenn neiċ ele in a láim ; aċṫ ċena iſ
in eſlaḃſa ſéʒṫaiſ inna haiſṫi ⁊ ní hi ſéṫ. Commao hé
in oeſmeſeċṫ híc "ní ṫeſcoa," aſ ſoṫuilleo "oa" ſoſſ
in ſocul ceſṫ : aċṫ ċena incſeċṫaſ ſein, aſ ní "oeiċneo"
iaſn oílſi ṫoſmaċ ſillaibi, aċṫ iſ "ſoſmolao ſileo ;" ⁊
iſ é ſo a oeiſmeſeċṫ ſioe :—

> Céim o loċaiḃ oo línn ól
> Co ʒloċaiḃ clú nao ʒano ón :
> Teċṫ ſeċ eoċu i cino ċſíce—
> Maiṫ beṫhu im biṫe annón.

Caoe oin in oeċneo iſ ino ſuno aṫſubſummaſ. "Lainn
ſiſ ⁊c. Nin. "Tenn" oo oénam oo'no ni aſ "ṫen" .i. ṫene,
aſ oaiʒ ʒo ſo[ḟ]ſeſſao oo "chenn" : ocuſ oéċneo iaſn
oílſi ſein. Iſ amlaio ſo, immoſo, oeſmeſeċṫaiʒṫiſ na
heſnaili-ſea in aluſ liḃuiſ .i. oiċneo amal aṫá "oochuſin"
.i. ṫellao a chenn oé .i. 'n "eṫ," aſ iſ "oocuiſ[i]neṫ" ſobui
ne ſſiuſ. Iſ e, immoſo, in oeiċneo, uṫ eſṫ "maelan" .i.
"án" in cenn ele : iſ é in cenonaċſoſ, uṫ eſṫ "ſenchaſ,"
aſ iſ "ſenchaſ" ſobúi oe ſſiuſ. Iſ e ſo incſeċhao nan
oeſmeſeċṫ-ſea .i. ni oiċneo iaſn oílſi oiʒḃáil ſillaibi ⁊ ni
oiċſeo iaſno ino aſ[ſ]aoe ciſeo aſile. Aſaill ano oan, iſ

off the word and without anything else in its place, as some
one said :

> A meeting I appointed—great the folly—
> In the stand above Druimm :
> O my Lord, O king of noble mysteries!
> .   -   .   .   . &c.

"Ru ra"—it is the example there ; for it is "run ran" that
was lawful. But the "bi-heading" is—two heads on it, that
is, its own head and another head ; and that its propriety
may be the doubling of the last letter of the word, as if
benn were made of what is *ben*, as is said :

> The desire of a man of battle [is] purple spoil ;
> God's fire comes gloomy, not rare ;
> A strong stroke [is] from a shaft of eight hands ;
> Usual a head in the fist of Cu of deadliness.

So that it be in matter the example may be here, that is,
his own head on that man, and the head of another one in
his hand ; but yet it is in speech these proprieties are
viewed, and not in matter. So that it be the example here,
"*ni tercda*," for "*da*" was added to the proper word ; but
yet that is criticized, for the increase of a syllable is not
"bi-heading" according to propriety, but it is a "superabundance of poets ;" and this is the example of that :

> Advance from lakes for a net of twists,
> With celebrities—a fame not narrow this :
> Coming past horses in the end of a territory—
> Good the life in which there is plentiness.

What, then, is the "bi-heading" in the round we have
spoken. "Lainn fir, &c." Not difficult. To make *tenn* of
that which is *ten*, that is, *fire*, with a view that it may
answer to *cenn*, and that is "bi-heading" according to
propriety. The following, however, is the way these
divisions are exemplified in other books, that is, "be-
heading" as is *dochusin*, that is, cutting its head off it ;
that is, the "et," for it is *docuis*[*i*]*net* it was formerly.
But the "bi-heading" is as is *maelan*, that is, *an* is the
other head : the "headlet-changing" is as is *senchas*, for it
is *fenchas* it was formerly. The following is the criticism
of these examples, that is, diminution of a syllable is not

íaτ na Focail ȝnáτα ınoıú "oocuṗın," ⁊ "maelán," ⁊
"ṗenchaṗ." Iaṗn aṗṗaτaıb oın aτα oeıṗmeṗecτα ṗunc :
aṗ ṗoṗταṗ ıaτ na Focail ȝnáττα acu ṗıoe "oocuıṗıneτ" ⁊
"mael" ⁊ "Fencaṗ." Iṗ é, ımmoṗo, ın cennaċṗoṗ ınoıu
"ṗenchaṗ" oo oenam oo'no [F]ocul aṗ "ṗenchaṗ :" aṗ ıṗ
é ın ȝnáτaċ ınoıu "ṗenchaṗ," uτ oıcıτuṗ :—

Féȝṗaıτ Fılın Fáıl ıṗoṗ
Fencaṗ co Feıȝ la Fenȝoṗ :
Mao íaṗ mal caċ maıȝe ımmaċ,
Ooṗṗóıṗce oóıne Oubτaċ.

"Fenaċaṗ :" ıṗ é ın oeṗmeṗecτ ann ṗeın .F. aṗ .ṗ. ano.
Iṗ cumma ooȝníτeṗ ı τoṗuċ ⁊ ın oeṗıuo Focuıl ın oíċneo
⁊ ın cennaċṗoṗ : ın oeṗıuo, ımmoṗo, Focuıl namma aṗ
ȝnáτ oóċneo oo oénam. Nı aıccem oan ıc Fıleoaıb na
Ȝaeoeılȝe aınm ṗáın Foṗ oíȝbaıl lıττṗı ⁊ ṗıllabı
amal aτċıam Foṗ τoṗmaċ lıττṗı ⁊ ṗıllabı .ı. "oóċneo"
τoṗmaċ lıττṗı ⁊ "Foṗmolao" τoṗmaċ ṗıllabı.

Oıα nıme nımReılȝe ıl luRȝ ın eıȝ-
τhıαR αR muıch oı á meıτ .ı. Aṗ ṗélao
Fıṗınnı aτbeṗ "Oía nıme," no oı á Fıṗ con naċ Oıa aṗ
íoal. "Nımṗeılȝe ıl luṗȝ nan oemına oc an oenταṗ éȝem
aṗ méτ am muıċe."

Oıα mαR mo αnαccol oe muR τeıno-
τıoe oı'u-oeRcn oe'R.ı. Móṗ-Oía oo mm 'anaccul
aṗ ımmeo ın τeneo, bale ı τeılȝıτıṗ oéṗa co cían ıc o
oéıcṗın .ı. aṗ Fıτ muṗ ımmeo, uτ oıcıτuṗ :

Múṗ ımmeo ταll ıṗ ıno ṗecτ,
Coṗ búaıo ıṗ bṗíaτhaṗ lán-cheṗτ :
Oú bale, oú oúτhaıȝ laτ,
Cul comeτ, ıṗ cul caṗṗaτ.

Oíu-oeṗc oan nomen comṗoṗṗıτum ó Laτın ocuṗ Scoτıc.

" beheading" according to propriety, and anything else is not " be-heading" according to the antiquity. Another thing in the case too—the usual words at present are—*dochusin* and *maelan*, and *senchas*. According to the ancients then examples are here ; for the usual words with them were *docuisinet*, and *mael*, and *fencas*. But the " head-changing" at present is to make *fencas* of the word which is *senchas ;* for the usual at present is *senchas*, as is said:

> The poets of Fal have viewed here
> The Fenchas with illumination by Fergus :
> If it is in reference to the poet of every plain forth—
> Dubthach has surpassed men.

" Fenachas :" the example there is *.f.* for *.s.* It is alike in the beginning or in the end of a word the " be-heading" and the " head-changing" are made ; but in the end only of a word it is usual to make the " bi-heading." We do not see again with the poets of the Goedelic a different name for diminution of a letter and of a syllable, as we see for increase of a letter and of a syllable, that is, " bi-heading" increase of a letter, and " superabundance" increase of a syllable.

THE GOD OF HEAVEN—MAY HE NOT ALLOW ME INTO THE HOST IN WHICH THERE IS CRYING ON ACCOUNT OF SMOKE FROM ITS GREATNESS .ı. For the manifestation of truth he says, " God of heaven," or from his knowledge that he is not a God who is an idol. " May he not allow me into the host of the demons, with whom crying is made on account of the greatness of their smoke."

GREAT GOD MY PROTECTION FROM THE FIERY RAMPART OF LONG EYES OF TEARS ! .ı.—Great God for my protection against the fence of the fire, a place in which are shed tears for a long time a-looking on it. That is, for mur means *fence* (*immed*), as is said :

> " Mur" [means] *fence* beyond in the law.
> " Coph," *victory,* and a full-right *word.*
> " Du" [means] *place,* " du" *inheritance* with thee.
> " Cul," *protection,* and "cul," *chariot.*

" Diu-derc" accordingly is a noun compounded from

Oiu .ı. ıncían : vepc .ı. púıl, uc oıxıc Ʒpánnı ınʒen Cop-
maıc ppı Fıno :

> Fıl oune,
> Rıpm [b]ao buoe lem oıu·vepc,
> Ap a cpıbpıno ın bıċ ule,
> Ɑ meıcc Maıpe, cıo oıúbepc!

OIA FIREN, FIROCUS, CLUINES MO OO. NU'AILL OO NIM·I'AĊ NEL

.ı. Oıa pípóen, no
Oía na pípén. "Fıp-ocup" .ı. quıa epc Oeup ubíque ec
ppope omnıbup ınuocancıbup eum. Mo oo-nuáıll .ı. mo
oo nuáıll .ı. núall mo cuıpp ┐ m'anma ıap nelaıb co íaċ
nıme : no, núall petap/laıce ┐ nu-pınao. No, "mo oo-
nuaıll" .ı. mo oó núall .ı. mo núall oó .ı. oo Oıa. bío oan
"íaċh" mıno ┐ "ıaċ" pepano, uc oıcıcup :

> Fó aınm oo maıċ ıp oo míao,
> Fí aınm o'ulc ıp o'anpíao :
> Ɑ'n Fíp ıp ní popup pano,
> I'aċh mıno ┐ íaċh pepano.

Latin and Scotic. "Diu," that is, *long;* "derc," that is, *eye:* as Granne, daughter of Cormac, said to Find:

> There is a person,
> For a long look at whom I should feel grateful,
> For whom I should give the whole world,
> O Son of Mary, what a privation !

GOD RIGHTEOUS, TRULY NEAR, WHO HEARS MY SAD WAIL TO THE HEAVEN-LAND OF CLOUDS .I.—Righteous God, or God of the righteous. "Truly near," that is, because God is everywhere, and near to all who invoke him. "Mo do nuaill," that is, my two wails; that is, the wail of my body and of my soul behind clouds to the land of heaven: or, the wail of the Old Law and of the New Testament. Or, "mo do nuaill," that is, "my to him wail," that is, my wail to him, that is, to God. "Iath," again, means a *diadem,* and "iath," a *territory,* as is said:

> "Fo" [is] a name for *good* and for *honor,*
> "Fi" [is] a name for *bad* and for *disobedience:*
> "An" [means] *true,* and it is no weak knowledge,
> "Iath" [is] a *diadem,* and "iath" is a *territory.*

amra choluim chilli.

[CAPITULUM I.]

DE MŒSTITIA OMNIUM RERUM IN MORTE COLUMBAE, VEL DE EXITU COLUMBAE.

1. Ni di[s] sceoil d'uae neill, .i. Ni cen scel, no ni dis in scél, no ní dis in scel d' Uíb Néill Colum Cille do éc: no, "d'Uae Néill" .i. do innui Néill. No, ni di[s] scéoil .i. ní dúṫe scéoil .i. ni ba scél do duid .i. cloṫaigfiter.

2. Ni uchtat oen-maige mor-mairg, mor-deilmn di[f]olaing, .i. Ni do oen maig as uch, no as íaċtad, aċt tóċis campis. Is mairg mór esteċt Coluim Cille. "Deilm" .i. is mor in crith ⁊ in cums[c]ugud tánic is inn Erind la hesteċt Coluim Cilli .i. ar fit deilm .i. torand, no ṫrost, ut dicitur:

Atá ben is tír,
Ni apar a hai[n]m,
Maidid esi a deilm,
Amal ċloiċ a tailm.

3. Ris re' asneid colum cen beiṫ, cen chill.

Ris nád fir,
O' ricfa co teċ a ríg:
Cóiċ bas lugu inn [d]ía sin
Inná Finnía find senċaid?

.i. Is di[f]olaing dún in scél is ind ré in aisnéter dún Colum Cille do ésteċt. "Cen bit" .i. cend a beiṫ im

THE AMRA OF COLUM CILLE.

[CHAPTER I.]

OF THE SORROW OF ALL THINGS IN THE DEATH OF COLUMBA, OR OF HIS DEPARTURE.

1. NOT A TRIFLE OF A STORY ABOUT THE DESCENDANT OF NIALL. .ı. Not without a story, or not trifling the story, or a poor thing is the story for the descendants of Niall—Colum Cille to die : or, " d'Uae Neill," that is, for the posterity of Niall. Or " ni di[s] sceoil," that is, not a folly of a story, that is, it is not a story about a fool, that is, it shall be celebrated.

2. SINGLE PLAINS SIGH NOT GREAT WOE, GREAT RINGING UNBEARABLE. .ı. It is not for one plain that sighing is, or that shouting is, but for all plains. A great woe is the death of Colum Cille. " Deilm," that is, great is the trembling and the commotion that have come into Eriu with the death of Colum Cille : for " deilm" means that is, *sound*, or *noise*, as is said :

> There is a woman in the land,
> I do not tell her name :
> Her ringing bursts out of her
> Like a stone from a sling.

3. WHEN THE TALE RELATES COLUM WITHOUT BEING, WITHOUT CHURCH.

> A tale which is not true :.
> When he will have come to the house of his king,
> Of what will he be less that day,
> Than Finnia fair, the sage ?

That is, the tale is unbearable to us in the time in which it is related to us that Colum Cille is dead. " Cen bith,"

D

biċ, no im beċaiṙ : "cen chill" .i. cen a beiċ i cill. Ríp .i.
pcél, uc epc in Immacallaim in ṙa Ṫúapaṙ .i. áil píż
pipi péṙi : no, im ḃpeċaiḃ Nemeṙ, uc ṙiciċup—ní ṙil
ṙáimi pipi .i. ní ḟil aippiciuṙ ṙáimi ṙo pcelaiḃ oca. No,
combaṙ eṙ baṙ choip anṙ—cen ṙíl ṙámi pípi .i. cen ṙíl
óeżiṙeċṫa in pcelaiżi : ap bíṙ pipi .i. pcelaiżi, uc ṙixiṫ
Copppe mac Eṫain ip inṙ áip ṙopiżni ṙo ḃpep mac
Elaṙan :

Cen ċolṫ ap cpáiḃ cepníne,
Cen żepṫ ḟepḃba ḟop an appa aċipni ;
Cen aṙba ḟip ḟoṙpuba ṙipopċi,
Cen ṙíl ṙámi pepi : pob pen ḃpippe.

⁊ ip í pein céṫ áep ṙopónaṙ in Epinn.

4. COI INṘIA ṘUI ṘO ? .i. Coi .i. quomoṙo :
"inṙia" [.i.] innippep .i. cia cpuċ innippep ṙúi ṙe ? No,
"cói" .i. conap .i. cia conaip innippep ṙúi ṙe ? No, pobo
ṙúi ceċ ṙune in a conṙelż-pom co Inṙía.

5. SCEO NERA. .i. Sceo ⁊ céo ⁊ neo cpí comac-
comail Żóeṙelże .i. ciṙ Nepa mac Mopainṙ, no Nepa
mac Finṙ-chuill a Síṙiḃ—ní ċóempaṙ a apnéip : no pobo
ṙúi piṙe in aċpéżaṙ Choluim Chilli.

6. IN FAIṪh ṘE' ṘEṘE SI'ON SUṘIOṪh,
IS NU NAṘ MAIR. .i. Ip nu aṫbaċh in faiċh Ṙé
popuṙepṫap ḟop ṙeip in Sioin nemṙai : no, ṙan in faiṫ
Ṙé noaipneṙeṙ in puṙiżuṙ biap in iaċ Sion : ño, in faiṫ
popuṙepṫap ḟop ṙeip Ṙé in Sion.

7. NI MARṪhaR LENṘ. .i. Ní mapṫhap ocunṙ ;
no, ni ḟil mópaċ ocunṙ hi peċṫ-pa ; no, ni ḟil nech ṙi ap
mópaṙ ocunṙ.

8. NI LES ANMA AR SUI, AR ṘONCON-
ṘI'AṪh. .i. Ni ḟil ocunṙ nech leppaiżep, no poillpiżep
app anmain i peċṫ-pa, ap aċpullái úain in faṫh cáin ap

that is, without his being in the world, or in life ; " cen chill," that is, without his being in a church. " Ris," that is, a *story*, as is in the Dialogue of the Two Sages : " A king's delight is smooth stories ;" or, in the Bretha Nemed, as is said, " Not a sufficiency of a company's stories," that is, he has not a company's delighting of stories. Or that it may be it that were right in it—" Cen dil dami risi" (without a sufficiency for a company's story-teller), that is, without a sufficiency for the entertainment of the story-teller : for " risi" means, that is, a *story-teller*, as Corpre mac Etain said in the satire he made for Bress, son of Elada :

Without fruit on branch of *cernine*,
Without a cow's milk on which a calf may grow,
Without a man's residence may he wander lightless;
Without a sufficiency for a company's story-teller :
>   Be it the prosperity of Bress !
And this was the first satire that was made in Eriu.

4. How will a simple one tell of him ? .¹. " Coi," that is, *how* : " india," [that is], *will tell* : that is, what manner will a simple one tell of him ? Or, " coi," that is, *way* : that is, what way will a simple one tell of him ? Or, every person was a simpleton in comparison with him to India.

5. Even nera. .¹. *Sceo* and *ceo*, and *neo*, (are) three conjunctions of Goedelic. That is, even Nera, son of Morand, or Nera, son of Find-choll, from the Sidè—he would not master the relation of it ; or, he was a simpleton in comparison of Colum Cille.

6. The prophet of God, who by sion took his seat, it is late he lived not. .¹. It is lately died the prophet of God, who took his seat on the right of the heavenly Sion : or again, the prophet of God who used to relate the sitting which will be in the land of Sion : or the prophet who took his seat on the right of God in Sion.

7. There is no magnifying with us. .¹. He is not magnified with us, or there is not a magnifying with us this time, or there is not any for our magnifying with us.

8. Soul's light, our learned one is not, for he has been hidden on us. .¹. There is not with us any who benefits or illuminates our soul in this time, for our learned

ꝛui. No, "conoio" .i. ꝛallim .i. inti noꝛailleo o ꝼoꝛcetul
bꝛéntaio aꝛ cinao ⁊ aꝛ taꝛgabal. No, ni leꝛaiꝃeno
aꝛn anmain aꝛ ꝛúi, aꝛ ꝼoꝼoilꝃeo eꝛono .i. conoi[tuꝛ].

9. CONRO'ETUR biu bath. .i. Inti nochoi-
neteo, no nocométao aꝛm biu aetbat: no inti nochoin-
eteo aꝛm biu co cain, atbat.

10. AR DONbath bo ARN AIRCENO a
DILꝃ[E] .i. Atbat aiꝛuno inti o'm ba iꝛceno aꝛn
áilꝃiuꝛ olíꝃthec, aꝛ oobeꝛeo oún cet ní ba ail oún co
ꝃliꝃtech. No, inti bá aiꝛceno ꝼꝛi aiꝛceꝛect aꝛn aolaiꝃe,
atbath.

11. AR DONbath ba ꝼiaoat ꝼoioiaim.
.i. Atbath eꝛuno inti nooꝼaiomiꝛ co aꝛ Ꝼiaoat .i. co
aꝛn Oia maith .i. aꝛ teꝃeo a ꝛꝛiꝛut ꝼoꝛ nem cet
oaꝛoáin.

12. ARA NI 'N ꝼISSIO ꝼRISbEREO OMNU
hUAIN. .i. Aꝛ ní beꝛeo inti oobeꝛeo ꝼiꝛ-ꝛít oún: no,
ꝼiꝛ áit co na bio imecla ocuno. No, in ꝼiꝛio téꝃeo úain
in l'a.

13. AR NI 'N TATHRIT DO SLUINEO ꝼOCUL.
ꝼI'R .i. Ní aitꝛeteno cocuno inti noꝛeteo úain ⁊ noꝛluineo
ꝼíꝛ ꝼocuil; no, ni tic oi áꝛ tatꝛeoꝛ .i. oi áꝛ ꝛéꝛuꝃuo.

14. AR NI 'N ꝼORCETLAIO ꝼORCANAO
TU'ATHA TOI. .i. Aꝛ ní maiꝛ in ꝼoꝛcetlaio nonꝼoꝛ-
canao na túata com bítiꝛ inn a toꝛt: no, noꝼoꝛcanao
túatha im oenam toi: no, in ꝼoꝛcetlaio noꝛoꝛcanao na
tuata bataꝛ im Tai .i. ainm ꝛꝛotha in Albain.

15. hUILE bITH ba hAE hE'. .i. Robo leꝛꝛeom
int ule bit. No oan iꝛ intíꝛect ꝼéꝃtaiꝛ ano .i. "hé" .i.
tꝛúaꝃ. .i. iꝛ tꝛúaꝃ atat atꝛebtaioe in betha ꝛobo leꝛ-
ꝛeom: iꝛ cꝛot cen céiꝛ iatꝛioe ⁊ iꝛ cell cen abaio.

16. IS CRUIT CEN CEIS, IS CELL CEN
AbAIO. .i. Céiꝛ ainm oo cꝛuit bic bíꝛ i comáitect
cꝛuite móꝛe hi comꝛinm: no, ainm oo'n oelꝃain bic

one has gone from us to a fair land. Or, " condio," that is, " *I salt*" : that is, he who used to salt from instruction the stench of our crimes and of our transgressions. Or, our learned one does not enlighten our soul, for he has been covered on us .ı. " conditus," (he has been buried).

9. WHO USED TO PRESERVE ALIVE, HAS DIED. .ı. He who used to indulge, or who used to guard our living, has died ; or, who used to kindly indulge our living, has died.

10. FOR HE HAS DIED ON US, WHO WAS OUR CHIEF FROM RIGHT. .ı. He has died on us, from whom was certain our lawful importunity, for he used to give us everything that was pleasing to us lawfully. Or, he who was sure for the commiseration of our vilenesses, has died.

11. FOR HE HAS DIED ON US WHO WAS GOD'S MESSENGER. .ı. He has died on us, whom we used to send to our *Fiada*, that is, to our good God : that is, for his spirit used to go to heaven every Thursday.

12. FOR THE SEER IS NOT, WHO USED TO ATTACK FEARS FROM US. .ı. For he brings not who used to bring knowledge of peace to us : or, quick knowledge, so that there be not terror with us. Or, the seer who used to go from us to Hi.

13. FOR THE REPREHENDER IS NOT, WHO USED TO EXPLAIN TRUTH OF WORDS. .ı. He re-runs not to us, who used to run from us, and used to explain truth of word : or, he comes not for our reprehension, that is, for making us wise.

14. FOR THE TEACHER IS NOT, WHO USED TO TEACH THE TRIBES OF TOI. .ı. For the teacher lives not, who used to teach the tribes until they used to be silent : or, who used to teach tribes about the making of silence : or, the teacher who used to teach the tribes who were around Tai : that is, the name of a river in Alba.

15. WHOLE WORLD—IT WAS HIS. .ı. The whole world was his. Or again, it is an interjection that is viewed in it ; that is, " he," that is, " *wretched*," that is : A wretched thing are the inhabitants of the world which was his ; a harp without a base-chord are these, and a church without an abbat.

16. IT IS A HARP WITHOUT A BASE-CHORD, IT IS A CHURCH WITHOUT AN ABBAT. .ı. *Ceis* is a name for a small harp which does be in accompaniment of a large

poptap in téit him muoe na cpote, no oo na coblaigib : no, ainm oo'n tpom-téc. No, ip í in ceip ip in cpuit ani congbap in letpino con a tétaib inti, ut oixit poeta— Rop mac Fino cecinit, no Fepéeptne File :

Ni celt ceip ceol oe cpuit Cpabtene

Co pelaptap pop pluagu puan-bap :
Conpept coibniup etep pceo Main
Mopiaet macoact Mopca :
Ɖa mo lé cech lóg Labpeio.
Ɖa binniu cec ceól in cpot,
Appete Laibpaio Loingpec Lopc :
Cia p'ba ooct pop pune in pi,
Ni pocelt ceip Cpaiptini.

Ppimum capitulum huic upque canitup.

[CAPITULUM II].

DE ASCENSIONE EIUS IN CŒLUM.

1. ATTRUIC ROARD TRA'Th Oé' COLUM CUITéCTA. .i. Atpapact co poapo Culum in tan tánic cuitecta Oé ap a ceno .i. angil Oé.

2. FINN-[F]ETAL FRESTAL. .i. Ip finn, no ip taitnemac in petal oi á táncatap fpeptal : no, ip finn in pío-[F]lait tánic i fpeptal Choluim Cilli .i. Axal aingel cum cetepip angelip.

3. FIGLIS FUT OA'l. .i. Oopigni figill in pot pobái im uita .i. oá cét oéc pleétan leip cac laí, act i pollomnaib tantum, comtap lépi a apnai tpían a bla-lin, ut oixit poeta:—

Glé, nolaigeo ip inn geim,
In a ligu bá móp-páet :
Slict a apna tpian a étac
Ɖá léip oánapéteo gáet.

harp in co-playing : or, a name for the small pin which holds the cord in the wood of the harp, or for the tacklings, or for the heavy chord. Or the *ceis* in the harp is, what holds the side-part with its chords in it, as the poet said— Ros Mac Find sang, or Fercertne the poet :—

The base-chord concealed not music from the harp of
    Crabtene,
Until it dropped sleep-death upon hosts :
It strew affinity between Main
And full-grown Moriaet Morca :
Greater with her than every price Labreid.
Sweeter than any music the harp,
Which delighted Labraid Loingsech Lorc :
Though sullen upon secrets was the king,
The base-chord of Craiptine concealed not.

The first capitulum is sung as far as this.

[CHAPTER II].

OF HIS ASCENT TO HEAVEN.

1. VERY HIGH ROSE GOD'S TIME COLUM OF COMPANY. .ı. Colum rose very high the time God's companies came to meet him .ı. God's angels.

2. BRIGHT-SHRINE ATTENDANCE. .ı. Bright is, or shining is the shrine to which they came an attendance : or, bright is the peace-prince who came to the attendance of Colum Cille ; that is, Angel Axal with the rest of the angels.

3. HE FIGULATED LONG AS HE WAS. .ı. He made *figulum* the length (of time) he was in life ; that is, twelve hundred prostrations by him each day, except in great festivals only, so that his ribs were manifest through his sheet, as the poet said :

Clear, he used to be in the sand,
    In his bed was much distress ;
The form of his ribs through his dress
    Was manifest when the wind would blow it.

4. bai sa'ezul-sneid. .ı. Robo zaпıc a раеzul
.ı. recтm bliaona recтmozac, uт oıхıт ın ғile :

Teoпa bliaona bóı cen lér
Colum ın a oub-pécleг :
Luıo co haınzlıb aг a cácт
laп ré bliaona recтmozac.

5. bai se'ım-sa'ch. .ı. ba becc a гaıc .ı. ba bec
oomeleo, no ba bec a haгao.

6. bai sab suıce cec oıno. .ı. Roba гab
oaınzen noгoao cechn [o]ıummuг, no пobo гuı-abb : no
гabb cec oenna .ı. ceca aıпecтa coг a пıcceo Colum
Cılle. No, ba гo-abb ı гuтemlácт cec beпlaı co clechı :
no, пobo neптmaп ıг ınт [ғ]uı̇ce co пıacт co cleтı.

7. bai oıno oc lıbur-leızoocт. .ı. Robo
oıno гoпceтlaoa leızıг Colum Cılle.
8. caıssaıs cı'r cu'aıch. .ı. Roгoıllгız, no
гoleгaız cıпı ┐ túacha. No, гolaг oe ın cíп cuaıo : no,
гolaгaгтaп ıг ın cıп cuaıo : no, гoleгaız ın cíп cuaıo :
no, гoпo laıг é.

9. leıs cuach occıoens. .ı. leггaızeг, no
гoıllгızıг : no, пobo leıг cuac occıoentıг .ı. Eпıu ┐ lпıг
bó ғınne ғoпг ıno [ғ]aпze .ı. cuтпuma гohol̇гız, no
гoleг-aıl aquılonem ┐ occıoentem.
10. coтro[m] las orıens. .ı. Cuтпumma
гoba leıг oпıenг ┐ occıoenг.
11. oc clerıb crı-ooćcaıb. .ı. Oc cleıпchıb
'n a cпıoıb ғoптchı : no, o na cleıпchıb coг na cпıoıb
ғoпcoıb гoғozlaım. No oan гoпo oócт a cпıoe ım
cleпcecт ғпı cac.
12. ғo' oı'bao. .ı. Maıc a epılcıu, aп ғıc oíbao
┐ bach ┐ ba ┐ тeme ıc гluı[n]o epılcen.
13. oe' aınzıl ıre assı[n]orochaıb. .ı.
Aınzıl Oé nıme ooveochaтaп aп a ceno ın тan conuaп-
zaıb.
Secunoum capıculum húc uгque.

4. HE WAS LIFE-SMALL. .1. His life was short, that is, seventy-seven years, as the poet has said:

> Three years was without light
> Colum in his black church:
> He went with angels from his prison
> After six years [and] seventy.

5. HE WAS OF SLENDER FOOD. .1. Little was his sufficiency, that is, little was what he used to consume, or little was the satisfying of him.

6. HE WAS CHIEF OF SCIENCE IN EVERY HILL. .1. He was a firm chief, who used to repel every haughtiness; or, he was a learned abbat; or, chief of every hill, that is, of every assembly to which he used to go, was Colum Cille. Or, he was a good abbat in the knowledge of every language to perfection; that is, he was mighty in the knowledge until he came to perfection.

7. HE WAS A FORT AT THE BOOK OF THE LAW LEARNED. .1. A fort of teachers of the law was Colum Cille.

8. HE INFLAMED COUNTRY, TERRITORY. .1. He illuminated or he benefited countries and territories. Or, the north country blazed from him; or, he blazed in the north country, or he benefited the north country; or, it was his.

9. THE WEST TERRITORY WAS HIS. .1. He benefited, or he illuminated; or, the territory of the West was his, that is, Eriu and Inis Bo Finne on the ocean: that is, alike he illuminated, or he benefited North and West.

10. EAST WAS EQUALLY HIS. .1. Alike were his East and West.

11. WITH COMPANIES HEART-RESERVED. .1. With clerics in their hearts gloomy: or, from the clerics with the learned hearts he learned. Or, again, his heart was reserved about clericising with every one.

12. GOOD EXTINCTION. .1. Good his death; for "dibad" "bath," and "ba," and "teme," are said in signification of *death*.

13. WITH GOD'S ANGELS ON HIGH HE DEPARTED. .1. The angels of the God of heaven who came to meet him when he ascended.

The second chapter as far as this.

[capitulum iii].

INCIPIT TERTIUM [CAPITULUM.]   TITULUS :   DE REGIONE AD QUAM PERVENIT COLUM CILLE, ⁊ DE PLURIBUS GRADIBUS EIUS.

1. Ra'nic axalu la arbriu archan-glu. ⒈ Ranic-rom co du ιτá Axal aingel : no, "axalu," .ı. auxilium. No, "axalu," .ı. na[n] imacalam .ı. pánic reom τír ın véncap immaccallaim .ı. molav na Tpínoτe, quia vicunτ hlpaphim ⁊ Sapaphim : "Sanccup, ranccup, ranccup Dominup Deup Sabaoτh." No "axalu" .ı. uca ⁊ rolu .ı. compuıvıguv ó Laτın ⁊ o Soevılg .ı. panıc-reom a oen-τoga .ı. nem. No, Axal nomen ınv aıngıl noaccallav Colum Cille, ⁊ quov erτ uepıup, uτ uemebaτ Uıcτop av Paτpıcıum. "La aıpbpıu" .ı. la immev, no la pluag.

2. Ra'nic iaτh nav avaıg accesτar. .ı. Ranıc ın fepanv náv aıcıτep avaıg eτep, aćτ luχ.

3. Ranic τi'r vo moise munemar. .ı. Ranıc ın τıp ı τoımnem-nı Moıpı vo bıτ, ap 'r ecnaıv cać anv. Ir coıp Moıpe vo bıτh anv ap a [f]ebap.

4. Ranic maıge mo's nav genetar ciuil. .ı. Inıv bep nem-genemaın céol, pev punτ pempep ın pe.

5. Nav esτeτ ecnaıve. .ı. Nav epleτ ecnaıve, quia malı pepıbunτ ın fuτupo ⁊ non bonı. No, nav epτeτ ecnaıve fpıı apaıle, quia omnep pepıcı punτ ın coelo : no, nı eτaτ ecnaıve a aıpneıp, No, nı eτpenv neć fpıı écnać. No, nı ćluıneτ ecnaıve níav, ap cıuep celep-τep offıcıo aupıum coppopalıum non ınvıgenτ, pev cogıτa-cıonep puap ınτpoppıcıunτ alτepuτpum.

[CHAPTER III].

THE THIRD [CHAPTER] BEGINS. THE TITLE: OF THE REGION
TO WHICH COLUM CILLE CAME: AND OF ITS SEVERAL
ORDERS.

1. HE HAS REACHED CONVERSATIONS WITH THRONGS—
ARCHANGELS. .1. He came to the place where Angel Axal
is, or, "axalu," that is, *auxilium* (help). Or, "axalu," that is:
" of the conversations ;" that is, he reached a land in which
conversation is made; that is, the praising of the Trinity,
because the Cherubim and Seraphim say, " Holy, holy, holy,
Lord God of Sabaoth." Or, "axalu," that is, *uca* (choice),
and *solu* (only) : that is, a composition from Latin and
from Goedelic : that is, he reached his only choice, that is,
heaven. Or, Axal is the name of the angel who used to
address Colum Cille, and what is truer, as Victor used to
come to Patric. " La airbriu," that is, " with a multitude,"
or " with a host."

2. HE HAS REACHED A TERRITORY WHERE NIGHT HE
SAW NOT. .1. He has reached the territory where night is
not seen at all, but light.

3. HE HAS REACHED A LAND FOR MOSES WE DEEM. .1.
He has reached the land in which we deem Moses to be,
for every one in it is a sage. It is right that Moses be in
it for his excellence.

4. HE HAS REACHED PLAINS WHERE IT IS A CUSTOM
THAT MELODIES ARE NOT BORN. .1. In which non-birth of
melodies is the custom, but they are always in it.

5. THAT SAGES DIE NOT. .1. That sages do not perish,
because the bad shall perish in the future, and not the
good. Or, that sages listen not to each other, because
all are learned in heaven ; or, sages are not capable of telling
of it. Or, no one listens to oppression. Or, sages hear
not a spirit, for the celestial citizens need not the office
of bodily ears, but they look into their thoughts the one
the other's.

6. ASRALA RI SACART SAECHU. .ı. Rola
ap ꝓı na racapc a ṙaechu : .ı. ın ampıp a ecpécca, uc
ꝺıcıcuꝣ : cꝓıꞃcıꞃ eꞃc anıma ꞃc.

húc uꞃque ceꝓcıum [caꝓıculum].

[caꝓıculum ıu.]

ET IN HOC QUARTO CAPITULO DE MARTIRIO EIUS
COMMEMORATUR.

1. ꞃocehaes ᵹaıꞃ combuıċ. .ı. Roċeꞃaꞃ-
caꝓ ıꞃ ın ᵹaꝓıc-ꝓé ꝓobuı ıꞃoꞃ, co ꝓobꝓıꞃecaꝓ caċ ꝼoꝓ
ꝺemon ꞃ ꝺomon.
2. báꞃı huꞌach ꝼꞃı ꝺemal. .ı. Roboı ꞃeom
co ꝓꞌbo húaċ hé ꝼꝓı ꝺemon. No, "ꝼꝓı ꝺemal" [.ı.] ꝼꝓı
ꝺee malı: no " ꝼꝓı ꝺe-mal" .ı. ꝼꝓı ꝓí nan ꝺemna .ı. "ꝺe"
oꞌnꝺí aꞃ ꝺemon," mál," .ı. ꝓí. No "ꝺemal" nomen ꝓꞃo-
ꝓꞃıum ꝺemonıꞃ nobıċ ıc aımꝓıᵹuꝺ Coluım Cılle ꝺoᵹꝓeꞃ.

3. ꝺı am bo ᵹoısce celebꞃaꝺ. .ı. ꝺı am
bo ċoı aꞃcuꝺa celebꝛaꝺ Colum Chıllı. No, ᵹoıꞃce aıꝓı
ꝼéın .ı. aıꝓec nochluneꝺ ın ꝺemon ᵹuch Colum Chıllı
ı[c] celebꝛaꝺ, nı lamaꝺ coꝓ ꝺe co caıꝓceꝺ ın celebꝛaꝺ :
ꞃ con ıaꝓꝼaıᵹcıꞃ ꞃcela ꝺó ıaꝓ ꞃeın o Cholum Chıllıu. No,
ꝓobo ᵹoıꞃce ᵹabala ꝺoꞌn ꝺemon ꝓobuı ıꞃ ın mac leᵹınꝺ ın
Aꝓꝺ Macha .ı. macc leᵹınꝺ nocheᵹeꝺ ꝺo mmnaı cléꝓıᵹ
anꝺ .ı. In can ꝺoᵹnícea celebꝛaꝺ ꞃ oꝓꝼꝛenꝺ ıꞃꞃ anꝺ
nocheᵹeꝺ cucı, co ꝓoaꝓıᵹ Colum Cılle ꝼechc anꝺ ın ꝺemon
ıc ꞃmécıuꝺ ꝼoꝓ ın mac leᵹın, co ꝓochaıꝓmıꞃc Colum
Cılle ımm ón mac léᵹınꝺ ꝺul ımmach. Robo ᵹoıꞃce
ᵹobála ꝺın ꝺe ꝺemon ċelebꝛaꝺ Coluım Chıllı anꝺ ꞃeın.

6. THE KING OF PRIESTS DISMISSED DISTRESSES. .ı. The king of the priests sent off his distresses: that is, in the time of his death, as is said, "my soul is sorrowful, and so forth."

Hither so far the third [chapter].

[CHAPTER IV].

AND IN THIS FOURTH CHAPTER COMMEMORATION IS MADE OF HIS MARTYRDOM.

1. HE SUFFERED SHORT UNTIL HE WON. .ı. He suffered in the short time he was here, until he broke battle on Devil and world.

2. HE WAS A HORROR TO THE DEVIL. .ı. He lived until he was a horror to the Devil. Or, to "De mal," [that is], to the God of evil: or, "fri de-mal," that is, to the king of the demons, that is, "de," from the word *demon;* "mal," that is, *king.* Or, "Demal" is the proper name of the demon that used to be tempting Colum Cille continually.

3. TO WHOM CELEBRATION WAS SUSPENSION. .ı. To whom the celebration of Colum Cille was a way of arresting. Or, a suspension on himself: that is, while the Devil used to hear the voice of Colum Cille at celebration, he would not dare a stir from him until he would finish the celebration: and until news used to be asked of him after that by Colum Cille. Or, it was a suspension of possession for the demon who was in the student in Ard Macha: that is, a student who used to go to a cleric's woman there. That is, the time celebration and offering used to be made, it is then he used to go to her, until Colum Cille on one occasion perceived the demon at beckoning on the student, so that Colum Cille made a prohibition about the student going out. The celebration of Colum Cille then at that time was a suspension of possession from the demon. For the space of a mile and half of a

Fri ré míle col leith míle ba follus guth Col. C. 1[c]
celebrad, ut dixit poeta :

> Son a gotha—Colum Cille,
>   Mor a binne úar cach cléir :
> Co cend cúic cet déc ceimmend,
>   Aidble remmend, ed ba réil.

4. **as a cheird cumachtaig.** .i. A cu-
machta a chleircecta dognid rom rein.

5. **CONROITER RECT ROBUST.** .i. Cain
ro[f]itir, no rochomét in recc ronairt. No, rochomet
recht .i. recctiuidnem : roburt .i. roburtur .i. ronairt
hé i comet dirgetad.

6. **ROFES RU'AIM, ROFE'S SE'IS.** .i. Rofer
roim a haidnaicte, no rofer ic Róim a ecna rom
⁊ a chrabud. Serr .i. ro-fir .i. fir ecnai ⁊ fáitrine. hin
[O]ún dan atberat araile eirreirge Choluim Chille do
bith, ut dixit poeta :

> hI' con ilur a mmartra
> Di am ba Colum coem-dalta :
> Dolluid erri fó deped,
> Conid Dún a ren-nemed.

7. **ROSUICHE DO' DA'MA DEACTA.** .i. Ro-
ruidiged do airte na deachta ar teged caé dardain ad
Dominum. .i. Rodamad dó ruithe na deachta : ó macc
Dé róetarrtar rein. No robo in deacc damtha
meic Dé.

8. **DERB DAG IM BA.** .i. Ir demin ir maic inc
éc docuaid : no, im ba i .i. maic im ba íriu.

9. **ba eola axaiN ainzel.** .i. ba eolac in
immaccalmaib aingel ; no, ba eolac in immaccallaim
u' angil danid ainm Axal.

10. **ARBERC bassil brachu.** .i. In brac
diummura dochúaid ind im mor-dáil Dromma Cetta,

mile the voice of Colum Cille at celebration was manifest,
as the poet said :

> The sound of his voice, Colum Cille's,
>   Great its sweetness above every company :
> To the end of fifteen hundred paces—
>   Vast courses—it was clear.

4. FROM HIS POWERFUL PROFESSION. .ı. From the power
of his clericship he used to do that.

5. FIRM HE PRESERVED LAW. .ı. Well he knew, or he
guarded the firm law. Or, he guarded law, that is, *rectitude :* "robust," that is, *firm :* that is, firm he in guard-
ing rectitude.

6. SEPULCHRE WAS KNOWN, WISDOM WAS KNOWN .ı. The
sepulchre of his burial was known : or, his wisdom and
devotion were known at Rome. "Sess," that is, "so-fis,"
(good knowledge), that is, knowledge of wisdom and of
prophecy. In Dun (Downpatric), again, some say the
resurrection of Colum Cille will be, as the poet has said :

> Hi with the multitude of its relics,
> Of which was Colum, beauteous disciple :
> He went out of it at last,
> So that Dun is his blessed church.

7. THE SCIENCE OF DEITY USED TO BE LAID DOWN FOR
HIM .ı. The speciality of the Deity used to be laid down
by him, for he used to go every Thursday to the Lord.
That is, the knowledge of the Deity was granted to him :
from the Son of God he received that. Or, he was in
deity the taught of the Son of God.

8. TRULY, GOOD IS THE DEATH. .ı. It is certain that good
is the death he departed : or, "im ba i," that is, good is this
death.

9. HE WAS SKILFUL OF CONVERSATIONS OF ANGELS. .ı.
He was skilful in conversations of angels : or, he was
familiar in conversation to an angel whose name is
Axal.

10. HE EXPOUNDED BASIL'S JUDGMENTS. .ı. The design
of pride that entered him in the great convention of Druim

conio aiṗi ṙein tuc báithin teṙtemain a baṙil oo
tṙóetao in oiumaiṙ.　No, noaiṗbiṗeo bṙetha bṙátha
a baṙil.

11. **aṙẑaiṙ ẑni'mu oe aoꝑsib—aiṙꝑṙib
aioblib aioꝑsib.** .i. ꝛoeṗẑaiṙ imme a menmain
oo bith inn a Oia in molao ooṗatṙat na ṙloiẑ ꝼaiṙ.
No, ṗoeṗẑaṗt ẑnimu Oé oe chaiꝑṙin nan immeon oub,
ouaꝑṙech ; ⁊ iṗ eo aṙẑaṗẑ oe ṙeom ṙein in teṙtemain a
baṙil, no na bṙetha.　"Aioꝑṙi" ainm in chiul, no in
cṙónain ooẑnítiṗ eṗmóṙ ꝼeṗn E'ṗeno in tan ṙin, cio eo
ooṙcanao immalle : ⁊ iṗ tṙiaṙ in ceol ṙin ooṗonṙat ꝼiṗ
Eṗeno oo Cholum Chilliu im móṙoáil Oṙomma Ceta
ṗoáṙ míao menman ino.

huc uṙque quaṗtum [capiculum].

DE SCIENTIA EIUS IN OMNI PARTE [HOC QUINTUM CAPITULUM].

1. **ꝛaith ꝛith ꝛethes.** .i. ꝛoṗaitheṙtaṙ, no
taṗṗaio oó in ṗith ṗoṗeteṙtaṙ.

2. **oaṙ cais ca'in-oenam.** .i. oo[ẑ]nío cain-
ẑním oaṗi ceno a miṗeṙen .i. aṗ ꝼit caiṗ .i. miṙcaiṗ.

3. **ꝼaiẑ ꝼeṙb ꝼithiṙ.** .i. Noꝼúaẑeo, no noꝼ́ẑeo
bṙethiṗ ino ꝼoṗcetail in ꝼéth-ataiṗ.　No, "ꝼithiṗ" .i. ṙíṗ,
no amnaṗ.　bio oan "ꝼeṗb" ic ṙlaino tṗí ṗét .i. "ꝼeṗb"
bṙiathaṗ, ut oicituṗ : "mao iaṗ ꝼeṗbaib ꝼíṗ-amṗaṗb
beṗlai biaṙ bain :' no, "iṗ ꝼaṗ ꝼénechaṗ ic ꝼeṗbaib Oé."
bio oan "ꝼeṗb" bolc, ut oicituṗ : "Tuṗcbait ꝼeṗba ꝼoṗ
a ẑṗuaoaib iaṗ cíl-bṙethaib" .i. iaṗ cloén-bṙetaib.　bio
oan "ꝼeṗb," ut oicituṗ : "théoṗa ꝼeṗba ꝼiṗa ooṙnacht,"
.i. ṗoṙimmaiẑ aṙṙal aṗ Moẑ Nuaoat.

Cetta, so that it is on account of that Baithine quoted a text from Basil for the subduing of the pride. Or, he used to expound the judgments of judgment from Basil.

11. HE FORBADE WORKS FROM CHORUSES—VAST THRONGS, CHORUSES. 1. He forbade, for his mind to be in God, the praising the hosts gave on him : or, he took charge of the works of God from the appearance of the black, hideous multitudes : and it is what excited that from him —the text from Basil, or the judgments. *Aidbsi* is the name of the music, or of the *cronan* most of the men of Eriu used to perform that time, whatever they would sing together : and it is through that music, which the men of Eriu made for Colum Cille in the great convention of Druim Cetta, pride of mind grew in him.

Hither so far the fourth [chapter].

[CHAPTER V.]

OF HIS LEARNING IN EVERY PART.

1. HE PERCEIVED THE COURSE HE RAN .1. He perceived, or the course he ran occurred to him.

2. FOR HATRED BENEFACTION. .1. He used to do benefit [in return] for hatred of him : that is, for "cais" means, namely, *hatred*.

3. THE TEACHER SEWED WORD. .1. The perception-father used to sow, or used to weave, the word of the doctrine. Or, "fithir," that is, *continual*, or *difficult*. "Ferb," again, is used to mean three things : that is, *ferb*, a word, as is said : "If according to the truly wonderful words of the white language it shall be :" or, "Fenechus is void beside the words of God." "Ferb" is also *bolc* (a bag, a blotch), as is said : "Blotches rise on his cheeks after crooked judgments," that is, after unjust judgments. "Ferb" also is, as is said : "Three white cows, he drove them off :" that is, Assal drove them on Mog Nuadat.

F

4. ჹаis ჹluаsа ჹlе'. .ı. bа ჹаr hé ıc eŗŗlocuð nа[n] ჹluаŗ : no ŗobo ჹаeṫ ŗum ıc ჹleoð ჹleŗeŗŗа. No ჹonаıŗ nа ჹlúаŗа co ჹlé .ı. eochаıŗ ჹlé Colum Cılle ðo ŗéðıჹuð ჹlúаŗ no ċeŗṫ.

5. ჹlınsıus sаlmu. .ı. Rоჹlınnıჹ nа ŗаlmu ŗо obıl ⁊ аŗṫŗıŗc ; no, ŗoŗoჹlаınð nа ŗаlmu.

6. sluınsıus lе'ჹ lıbRu, lıbuıR uттаR саsеоn. .ı. Rоŗluınneŗṫаŗ nа ŗаlmu ıc а ṫıċṫаın ıаŗŗ а ŗoჹlаım, ⁊ ıŗ úаŗ ın ŗluınn, ŗıuŗ ŗо ıŗın. No, ŗıc : ŗoŗluıneŗṫаŗ lıbŗu leıჹ .ı. ınð ŗeċṫа, аmаıl ŗoċа-ŗаŗṫаŗ lıbŗu Еoın Саŗéoın. No, ní ŗ'bo mo leıŗŗ lıbuıŗ ınð ŗechṫа ðo ṫıаcṫаın quаm lıbuıŗ Еoın Саŗŗeoın : no, ŗoleჹ Еoın Саŗŗıoın lıbŗu leჹıŗ.

7. саṫhа ჹulаe ჹаelаıs. .ı. Rоჹаılаŗṫаŗ саṫhа ın cŗóıŗ. No Сúlаı аŗ mаıṫ аnð .ı. ŗobŗıŗ cаth nа ṫŗí Сúl .ı. cаṫ Сúlı Ðŗemnı ŗоŗ Соnnаċṫu, ⁊ cаth Сulı Ŗeðа ŗоŗ Соlmаn Моŗ, mаc Ðıаŗmаcа, ⁊ cаch Сulı Rаṫhın ŗоŗ Ulṫu ıc coŗnаm Roıŗ Тоŗoċhаıŗ eṫeŗ Соlum Сılle ocuŗ Соmჹаll. No, ჹálаıŗ, ŗobŗıŗeŗṫаŗ, uṫ ðıxıṫ poeṫа :

> Móŗ ðo chаṫаıb ჹаelаŗṫаŗ,
> Ŗоŗ [а] аṫhаıŗ ŗаlаŗṫаŗ :
> Mаcc ın mаıl а mаın-mаŗṫen,
> Ŗí ŗeŗ Ŗаıl аðаჹаŗṫаŗ.

8. lıbRu sоlmаn sеxus. [.ı.] No, ŗoŗıаch lıbŗu Solmаn. No, ŗexuŗ .ı. ŗeჹıuŗ, uṫ ðıcıṫuŗ ŗenchаŗ ŗŗo ŗenchаŗ.

9. sınа sсео ımRımа Rаıch.—Imŗımа .ı. ðonennа ⁊ onðí аŗ ımbéŗ аṫá ımŗımа : "ŗаıch," .ı. ŗо-ŗаıðeŗṫаŗ ŗeın .ı. ðoucаð ın ṫаn ṫıcŗаð ŗoненð ⁊ ðoненð.

10. RАNNАıs RАınð со ŗıჹuıR Е́ТЕR lıbRu lе'ჹ. .ı. Rоŗаnnаŗṫаŗ ŗаınð co ŗıჹuıŗðаchṫ eṫeŗ lebnаıb ınð leჹınð, no ınð ŗechṫа .ı. noðelıჹeð а ŗṫаıŗ ⁊ а ŗıаŗ ⁊ а mоŗoıl ⁊ аn аноჹаıჹ.

4. HE PROBED GLOSSES CLEAR. .ı. He was active at the resolving of the glosses: or, he was keen at deciding of conflicts. Or, he probed the glosses clearly: that is, a clear key was Colum Cille for unravelling of glosses, or of questions.

5. HE ILLUSTRATED PSALMS. .ı. He illustrated the psalms under obelisk and asterisk: or, he learned the psalms.

6. HE EXPLAINED THE LAW'S BOOKS—BOOKS WHICH CASEON LOVED. .ı. He explained the psalms at his understanding of them after the learning of them: and above the explanation: poetry under that. Or thus: He explained the Books of *Leg*, that is, of the Law, as Eoin Caseon loved books: or, of no greater importance was it with him to understand the books of the Law, than the books of Eoin Caseon: or, Eoin Caseon read the books of the Law.

7. HE FOUGHT THE BATTLES OF THE STOMACH. .ı. He fought the battles of the gluttony. Or, " Culai" is what is good in it: that is, he broke the battle of the three *Cul's*, that is, the battle of Cul Dreimne on the Connachta, and the battle of Cul Feda on Colman Mor, son of Diarmait, and the battle of Cul Rathin on the Ulaid, at the contesting of Ros Torathair between Colum Cille and Comgall. Or, " galais," *he broke*, as the poet has said:

> Much of battles he broke,
> On [his] father he poured :
> The son of the chief from Main-Maistiu,
> The king of the men of Fal much dreaded.

8. THE BOOKS OF SOLOMON HE PURSUED. [.ı.] Or he pursued the books of Solomon. Or, " sexus," that is, "*fegius*," (he examined), as *senchas* (law) is said for *fenchas*.

9. SEASONS AND STORMS HE PERCEIVED.—" Imrima," that is, " storms," and from " imber" (shower) imrima is. " Raith," that is, he perceived that. That is, he used to understand when calm and storm would come.

10. HE DIVIDED DIVISION WITH FIGURE AMONG THE BOOKS OF THE LAW. .ı. He divided division with figuration between the books of the reading, or of the Law. That is, he used to separate their history, and their sense, and their moral, and their anagogue.

11. **Leʒais Rune Rochuaid eter sco-**
laib screptra. .ı. Roleʒ púne ın pořuche co fıcıř
na púne ın ꞇan ꞎobuı eꞇeř ꞎꞇolaıb ıc foʒlaım na ꞎꞇeꞎeꞎ-
ꞇřa. No, "ꞎořualꞇ" .ı. aınm do ꞇeıꞎꞇ bíř ıř ınd [f]aıꞎcı,
⁊ ıꞎ ıaꞇ ꞎo a aıꞎde řıde .ı. In ꞇan ꞎcear ⁊ a aʒed
fřı ꞇıř, domma ⁊ ꞇeꞎca ıꞎ ın ꞇíꞎ řın co cend řeꞝꞝm
blıadna, no ıꞎ ın blıadaın řın namma : mad řúaꞎ, domma
⁊ moꞎꞇlaıd ıꞎ ınd aeoꞎ řın : mad říꞎ, domma ⁊
moꞎꞇlaıd foꞎ míla ın maꞎa. Noınnıřed ıaꞎum ꞎuna ınd
anmannaı řın do doınıb, com beꞇıꞎ ınn a foımꞇın. Roꞎualꞝ
dan ann maıle [aınmn aıle ?] do'n beıꞎꞝ řın.

12. **sceo ellachꞇ ımmuaımn eıscı**
ımm Rıth. [.ı.] Sceo .ı. ocuꞎ. Roellʒed acce ꞎeom
cohuaım ꞎeꞝha eꞎcı ım ꞎıꞝ ʒꞎéne .ı. eꞎcı ꞎıa ʒꞎéın o ꞎꞎím
co cuıcıd déc, ⁊ íaꞎ ʒꞎéın o chúıcıd déc co ꞎꞎím.

13. **Raıth Rıth la ʒReınn ʒescaıʒ.** .ı.
Roꞎo ꞎeıd dó eolaꞎ ꞎeꞝha eꞎcaı la ꞎıꞝh na ʒꞎene ꞝaıꞝ-
nemche. Iꞎ aıꞎı aꞎbeꞎaꞎ "ʒeꞎcaꞝ" fꞎı ʒꞎéın, aꞎ ıꞎ uaꞝhı
aꞝá ꞎollꞎı do na ꞎennaıb aılıb.

14. **SCEO RE'IN-RITh.** .ı. Robo éolaꞝ ıꞎ ꞎıꞝ ꞎénıꞎ
.ı. maꞎıꞎ. No, commad "ꞎían" bad choıꞎ and, uꞝ dıxıꞝ
Fınd hu baıꞎcne :

        Scél lém dúıb : doꞎdaıd dam,
        Snıʒıd ʒaım, ꞎoꞎaıꞝh řam :
        Ʒáeꞝ aꞎd, huaꞎ, ířel ʒꞎıan,
        Ʒaıꞎ aꞎꞎıꞝh, ꞎuꞝhach ꞎían.

        Roꞎuad ꞎaꞝ ꞎocleꞝh cꞎuꞝh,
        Roʒab ʒnaꞝh ʒıuʒꞎand ʒuꞝ :
        Roʒab uachꞝ eꞝe én,
        Aıʒꞎe ꞎé, e, moꞎclé.
                Scél lem duıb.

15. **Rımfeıꞝh Rınd Nıme Nech ınꞝoı**

11. HE READ THE MYSTERIES OF THE GREAT REVELATION AMONG SCHOOLS OF SCRIPTURES. .1. He read the mysteries of the great wisdom, until he knew the mysteries, the time he was among schools at the learning of the Scriptures. Or, "Rosualt," that is, a name for a monster which is in the ocean, and these are its signs. The time it belches and its face towards land, poverty and scarcity in that land till the end of seven years, or in that year only: if it is upwards, poverty and mortality in the air that: if it is downwards, poverty and mortality on the animals of the sea. He used to relate afterwards the mysteries of that animal to people, that they might be in suspicion of him (on their guard against him). *Rosualt* accordingly is another name for that monster.

12. AND HE HARMONIZED MOON'S CO-CIRCLE IN REGARD TO COURSE. [.1.] "Sceo," that is, *and*. The co-circle of Moon's course about Sun's course was harmonized with him: that is, Moon before Sun from prime to fifteenth, and after Sun from fifteenth to prime.

13. HE PERCEIVED (ITS) RACE WITH BRANCHING SUN. .1. Easy for him was the knowledge of Moon's race with the race of the radiant Sun. It is why *branching* is said to Sun, because it is from it illumination is for the other constellations.

14. AND SEA-COURSE. .1. He was skilful in the course of "renis," that is, "*of the sea.*" Or, that it may be "rian" that was right in it, as Find hU Baiscne has said :

> A tale I have for you. Ox murmurs,
> Winter pours, summer is gone :
> Wind high, cold : sun low ;
> Cry is attacking, sea resounding.
>
> Very red raying has concealed form,
> Voice of geese [barnacles] has become usual :
> Cold has caught wings of birds ; .
> Ice-frost time : wretched, very wretched.
>   A tale I have for you.

15. HE WOULD COUNT THE STARS OF HEAVEN, THE

cechn oinuais o chollum chilliu
cualamar. .i. No aipmebao petlanna nime inti
noinnippeo caċ ní póucop pochualamman o Cholum
Chille : no, noinnippeo Colum Cille oi a tpiallao
pohúaip oo pennaib.

huc urque quintum [capitulum].

---

capitulum ui.

DE ADMIRATIONE ET CARITATE EIUS HOC SEXTUM
CAPITULUM.

1. coich boi, coich bí'a beo baoib
amraoair ar iathaib iroocht ir-
thuaith. .i. Coich poboí, no cñich biap beó bao
chomuapal fiip, ná bao fíp-fontchiu fop fepannaib in
típ túaich? "Ap iathaib iroocht" .i. bá epoóct fpia
thuaithib no chíp aneċtaip, in tan conucaib a chill hi
topuċ .i. Eu : "Iptuaiċ" .i. fpim anthuaich. No "iroóct"
.i. ba epoóct hi tuaiċ .i. ba oóct a ċobaip peom fpi nech :
no, ba oocht im chobaip neich.

2. aofet co nu' nech nao ꝫoi' ꝫeoin.
.i. Noaipneoeo copici nú inti na aithꝫéoin ꝫoi ano fein.
No, ao "Fet" fil ano, ioem et uetup teptamentum, ꝝ
an "nu" ip Nouum Teptamentum .i. noaipneoeo oun
Fetaplaic co Nú-fiaonaipe, ut oixit anꝫelup, uel mona-
chup :

Maccán umal, atbep cet,
Oeup ei inoulꝫet :
Fopiꝫella Nú ocup Fet,
Im bethaio puthain pupꝫet.

PERSON WHO WOULD EXPOUND EVERY EXCEEDINGLY NOBLE
THING WE HAVE HEARD FROM COLUM CILLE. .ı. He would
count the stars of heaven the person who would relate
every very choice thing we have heard from Colum
Cille : or, what Colum Cille would tell about his very
high travelling to the stars.

Hither so far the fifth [chapter].

CHAPTER VI.

ABOUT THE ADMIRATION OF HIM AND ABOUT HIS CHARITY
THIS SIXTH CHAPTER.

1. WHO WAS, WHO SHALL BE ALIVE, WHO WAS MORE
WONDERFUL OVER TERRITORIES THAN THE VERY
LEARNED ONE OF THE NORTH-EAST ? .ı. Who was, or who
shall be alive, who was co-noble with him, or who was
more truly-learned over the territories of the north
country ? "Ar iathaib irdocht," that is, he was very
reserved towards territories, or external country, the time
he raised his church at first, that is, *Eu* (Hi) : "irthuaith,"
that is, facing me on the north. Or, "irdocht," that is,
he was reserved in a territory ; that is, reserved was his
association with any one, or he was reserved about the
association of any one.

2. HE USED TO DECLARE TILL LATELY ONE WHO KNEW
NOT GUILE. .ı. He used to relate until lately he who knew
not guile in himself. Or, it is "Fet," that is in it, the same
as *Old Testament*, and the "Nu" is *New Testament :* that
is, he used to relate to us *Veter Lex* (Old Law) with *New
Witness*, as an angel has said, or a monk :

An humble lad, prophecy says,
God to him will be kind :
He will testify *Nu* and *Fet*,
In life eternal he will rise.

3. ʒꞃess ꞃoꝼeꞃ ꝼechcnaċu. .ı. Roʒꝑeꞃꞃaıʒ, no ꝓochemnıʒ ımmalle ꝼꞃıꞃ na ꝼıꝑu .ı. aınʒıl. No, ꞃıc .ı. ba ꝼechcnaċu caċ ʒꞃeꞃꞃ ın ʒꞃéꞃꞃ ꞃoꝼeꞃaꞃcaꞃ Colum Cılle.

4. ꝼꞃı a'ꞃchu aꞃ chacꞃu co ꝺomun ꝺꞃınʒcıeꞃ. .ı. Ꝼꞃı aꞃaꝺu na cacꞃach uaıꞃlı ꞃoꝺꞃınʒeꞃcaꞃ: "co ꝺomun" .ı. co ꝑ'ba ꝺ ó aꞃomáın: no, "co ꝺo mun" .ı. co ꝺá ꞃomaın .ı. cuıꞃꝓ ocuꞃ anma : no, "co ꝺomun" .ı. aꝺ coelum. No, "ꝼꞃı aꞃchu aꞃ ċacꞃu" .ı. aꞃ chacıꞃ nıme, co ꞃuꝺꞃebꞃaınʒ ın ꝺomun ꝼꞃı ꝼıꝺıꞃı ꞃıaʒla ⁊ ꝺıꞃmıꞃeċca noeb; aꞃ ıc áꝑıꝺ ꝺoʒaıꞃceꞃ, uc ꝺıcıcuꞃ : "ꞃcale uel coelı ꞃunc ꞃanccı."

5. aꞃ ꝺeo ꝺoenachcha .ı. Aꞃ ꝺ[o]enachc meıc Ꝺé ꞃocheꞃaꞃcaꞃ .ı. co ꞃaʒbaꝺ ʒꞃeım ꝺó ceꞃaꝺ meıc Ꝺé. No, aꞃ Ꝺıa ꝺoʒnıꝺ ꝺoenaċc .ı. cıꝺnacul neıch aꞃ Ꝺıa.

6. aꞃ [ṡ]assa'ıb ꞃıʒcıeꞃ .ı. Iꞃ aıꝑı ꝺoʒnıꝺ ꞃom aꞃ ꝼáꞃaꝺ ꝺó ıꞃ ınꝺ ꞃıchıuꝺ huaꞃal.

7. ꞃıꞃıꞃ accobuꞃ a sula .ı. Roꝑec aꞃ Ꝺıa caċ ní ꝑob' accoboꞃ ꝑı ae ꞃuíl : na mná ⁊c.

8. suı slan cꞃeas cꞃısc .ı. In lán-ꝼuı ꞃen ꞃocꝑeceꞃcaꞃ Cꞃíꞃc : no ꞃlan cen ꝑheccaꝺ : no, " cꞃeıꞃ" .ı. a neꝑbo " cꞃeꞃco" .ı. ꞃoꞃoꞃbꞃeꞃcaꞃ ıaꞃum ı Cꞃíꞃc : no, ꝺoꞃac Cꞃíꞃc ꝼoꞃbaıꞃc ꝼaıꞃ.

9. ceo nı coıꞃm, ceo nı seꞃc oll-saıċ : seċnaıs beoıl .ı. Ocuꞃ nı ebeꝺ coıꞃm, no nı caꞃaꝺ coıꞃm, ⁊ ní ꝑ'bo ꞃeꞃcaꝺ leıꞃ co oll-ꞃaıch : ꝺoꞃechnaꝺ ꝺan ın beoıl.

10. baı caċh, baı casc .ı. Robaı cach, no ꞃoboı caċ .ı. Cacholıcuꞃ.

11. baı caꞃchaıc. .ı. Cóıc : lán ꝺo ꝺéıꞃc eꞃeom ulı. No, ꝼıċche Colum Cılle ó ꝺeꞃeıꞃc.

12. clochonꝺ oc buaıꝺ. .ı. Robo aıl ı caċ he oc bꞃeıċ buaꝺa ꝺo caċ. No, " cloch-onꝺ," .ı. cloċ

3. A COURSE HE MADE MOST FORTUNATE. .ı. He walked, or he stepped together with the white, that is, angels. Or thus: More fortunate than every course was the course Colum Cille made.

4. WITH THE CHARIOTEERS OF GREAT-CITY TO PROFUNDITY HE WAS BROUGHT. ı. With the charioteers of the noble city he ascended : "co domun," that is, until its good gift was for him. Or, "co do mun," that is, to two good gifts, that is, of body and of soul : or, "co domun," that is, to heaven. Or, "fri arthu ar chatru," that is, to the city of heaven, that he might bring the world to the ways of rules and examples of saints, for it is ladders they are called, as is said : "the saints are ladders even of heaven."

5. BEFORE GOD MADE MAN. .ı. For the humanity of the Son of God he suffered : that is, so that a persecution to him used to be the suffering of the Son of God. Or, for God he used to practise humanity, that is, the bestowal of a thing for God.

6. ON HIGH HE WAS KINGED. .ı. It is why he used to do that, with a view to satisfaction for him in the noble heaven.

7. HE YIELDED THE DESIRE OF HIS EYES. .ı. He exchanged for God every thing which was a desire to his eye : the women, and so forth.

8. A PERFECT SAGE, WHO BELIEVED CHRIST. .ı. The blessed full-sage who believed Christ ; or, perfect without sin. Or, "creis," that is, from the verb *cresco* (I increase): that is, he increased afterwards in Christ, or Christ gave an increase on him.

9. AND HE DESIRED NOT ALE, AND NOT A GREAT SUFFICIENCY: HE AVOIDED FLESH. .ı. And he used not drink ale, or he used not love ale, and it was not with him a desire as far as a great sufficiency ; he also used to avoid the flesh.

10. HE WAS LEARNED, HE WAS CHASTE. .ı. He was learned, or, "roboi cath," that is, a Catholic.

11. HE WAS CHARITABLE. .ı. Whole : full of charity he all : or, Colum Cille used to be boiled from charity.

12. A ROCK AT VICTORY. .ı. He was a rock in battle at bearing away of victory from every one. Or, "cloth-ond," that is, a stone of subduing, for "ond" is a stone. A

G

cloıchı, aп ꝼıc onꝺ cloch : ꝛobo cloċ ıaꝛum cloıchı caċ
uılc Colum Cılle.

13. ьоɪ ɫeꞅ ɫɑ'ɴ. .ı. ьo eꝛeom co cabꝛaꝺ a lán-
leꝛ ꝺo caċ.

14. ьоɪ ɫeoꝛ-ɫeꞅ оɪȝeꝺ. .ı. ꝛobo leoꝛ nole
ꝛaıȝeꝺ aeȝeꝺu.

15. ьоɪ оьеɪꝺ. .ı. auıꝺuꝛ .ı. laınꝺ.

16. ьаɪ huɑꞅɑɫ, ьоɪ huɑꞅ ɑ ьɑ'ꞅ. .ı. ьa
ꝼoꝛcaıl ꝼoꝛ baꝛ .ı. ꝼoꝛ ꝺıabul, no peccaꝺ : no, ꝛob' uaıꝛ
a báꝛ : no, ꝛoꝛıcıꝛ báꝛ uaꝛa.

17. ьоɪ ɫɪeɴ. .ı. ɫemꝛ .ı. aılȝen.

18. ьоɪ ɫɑ cꝛɪꝺe cech ecɴɑꝺɑ. .ı. ꝛobo
lıaıȝ leꝛaıȝche cꝛıꝺe cach ecnaꝺa : no, ꝛobo chaımꝛıȝche
ꝺo ꝛeıꝛ cꝛıꝺe cec ecnaꝺa : o'nꝺı aꝛ lıȝo .ı. cumꝛıȝım.

19. ɑꝛ mɪɴꝺɴ ɑχɑɫ ɴɑcɑɫɫɑꝺ. .ı. aꝛn
úaꝛal no aıcelleꝺ ınn aınȝel ꝺı a ꝛ'bo aınm aχal : no,
"ıaꝛ mınꝺn aχaln accallaım" .ı. ıaꝛn acallaım ꝺé
ꝺo-ꝛom : aꝛ ıꝛ éꝺ mınꝺn aınȝel cꝛıꝛc macc ꝺé. No, an
aꝛ ꝺech ꝺe aınȝlıb—ba menıc ꝺo ꝛım an accallaım ꝛıꝺe:
ba canaıꝛı ꝺan ꝺo accallaım aınȝel a acallaım ꝛeom.

20. ьɑ ɑɪɴmɴe ɑꝛ ɑm ьeьɑ. .ı. ꝺo ꝼcaıꝺ
acbaċ .ı. ꝺo luȝu ꝺıȝe acbach : aꝛ nı ċaıꝺeꝺ lınꝺ na
bıaꝺ ıꝛ ın blıaꝺaın acbach, aċc ı Saċuꝛnꝺ, no ın ꝺom-
mnuch.

21. ьɑ' ьɪɴꝺ. .ı. ьá bınꝺ a ȝuch ı[c] celebꝛaꝺ.

22. ьɑ о'eɴ ɑ cheꝛꝺ cɫeɪꝛchechcɑ. .ı.
ꝛobo en ꝺı a elaꝺnaıb cleıꝛchechc : aꝛ ba ꝛuı, ba
ꝼáıch, ba ꝼıle. No, ꝛobo leoꝛ ꝺo caċ ınꝺ oén-ċeꝛc
ċleıꝛċechca baí oca, uc ꝛacꝛıcıuꝛ ꝺıχıc :

ȝenꝼıꝺ maccan ꝺı a ꝼıne,
ьıꝺ ꝛuı, ьıꝺ ꝼaıch, ьıꝺ ꝼıle :
Inmaın leꝛbaıꝛe ȝlan, ȝlé,
Naꝺ ebeꝛa ımmaꝛbé.

23. ьɑ ꝺо ꝺоɪɴɪь ꝺɪꞅcꝛuCɑɪɴ. .ı. ьa anꝛa
ꝺo ꝺoıꝛıb ꝛeꝛúcan a ȝnım ꝛon. No, commaꝺ "ꝺıꝛcꝛéıc"

stone then of the subduing of every evil was Colum Cille.

13. HE WAS A FULL BENEFIT. .i. He was, so that he used to give his full benefit to every one.

14. HE WAS AN ABOUNDING BENEFIT OF GUESTS. .i. It was much he used to benefit guests.

15. HE WAS AVID. .i. "Avidus," that is, eager.

16. HE WAS NOBLE, HIGH WAS HIS DEATH. .i. He was superior over death, that is, over the Devil, or sin ; or, his death was high ; or, he knew death over him.

17. HE WAS GENTLE. .i. "Lenis," that is, gentle.

18. HE WAS A PHYSICIAN OF THE HEART OF EVERY SAGE. .i. He was a physician of the benefiting of the heart of every sage : or, he was bound according to the heart of every sage ; from that which is "ligo," that is, *I bind.*

19. OUR DIADEM WHO USED TO CONVERSE WITH AXAL. .i. Our noble who used to converse with the angel, whose name was Axal. Or, "iar mindn axaln acallaim" (after the diadem of angels' conversation), that is, after conversation with God by him : for Christ, Son of God, is the diadem of angels. Or, what is best of angels—frequent of number was the conversation of these : second, accordingly, to the conversation of angels was his conversation.

20. IT WAS ABSTEMIOUSNESS ON ACCOUNT OF WHICH HE DIED. .i. Of thirst he died, that is, from littleness of drink he died : for, he used not to take ale or food in the year he died, but in Saturday, or in Sunday.

21. HE WAS MELODIOUS. .i. Melodious was his voice at celebration.

22. HIS PROFESSION OF CLERICSHIP WAS ONE. .i. Cleric-ship was one of his sciences, for he was a sage, a prophet, and a poet. Or, abundant for every one was the one pro-fession of clericship which he had, as Patric said :

A child will be born of his tribe,
He will be a sage, will be a prophet, will be a poet :
Beloved the pure, clear lamp,
Who will not speak deceit.

23. HE WAS TO PERSONS INSCRUTABLE. .i. Difficult for persons was the conception of his deeds. Or, it may be

bao chóip ano .i. Ni cluineo pepeic oune in bale in
oénao a cpabuo .i. ip in oicpub, no ip in oub-peclep.

24. ba oi'n oo nochcaib. .i. Imm écac.

25. ba oio oo bochcaib. .i. Immi biao.

26. ba nua nochesao cach cromm-
oi o pochuch. .i. Cac cpom-pocac no chépao—ba
amal núa leip-peom pein. No, "ba cpuimmiu cac
[p]ochaig oún in cepao nua-pa," ap in oall.

27. o cholum cosc cuach. .i. O Cholum
nochoipcíp na cúacha.
28. miao mar munemar mann. .i.
Ciagmaic in a munigin in mop-aipmicnig pin im nem
oúinn. No, oommunem oobepchap aipmiciu móp oo oo
chino na[n] gnim po. "Miao maip" .i. imbeo manna .i.
in maino. Ip eo acbepcíp meicc Ippael ppi a manchu
.i. Cluio epc hoc nipi cibup celepcíp? Oommuinimap íapum
oobepcap apmiciu mop in bío nemoa oo-pom.

29. noogeilsigpe crisc ecer olig-
cecu. .i. Nongeba pom Cpípc in a geilpine .i. in a
muncepap ecep na oligchechu [.i.] ecep aingliu ocup
apch-aingliu.
30. trias na cí'ana cocaislia. .i. Cpip
in pé cian pobui ic caipleo ipop .i. oc cpabuo.

[capiculum uii.]

DE PRUDENTIA EIUS ET LECTIONE ET SAPIENTIA.

1. ergnaio sui siacc slicht cetrair.
.i. Ip cpgna in pui popiacc plicc na cccpi puiacc.

" discreit" (cryless) is what is right in it : that is, the place in which he used to make his devotion used not to hear the cry of a person : that is, in the desert, or in the Black Church.

24. HE WAS A SHELTER TO NAKED. .ı. In regard to clothing.

25. HE WAS A CONSOLATION TO POOR. .ı. In regard to food.

26. IT WAS [AS] NEW HE USED TO SUFFER EVERY HEAVINESS FROM ATTACK. .ı. Every heavy attack he used to suffer—that was like a new one with him : or, "heavier to us than every attack is this new suffering," says the Blind (that is, Dallan).

27. FROM COLUM DISCIPLINE OF TERRITORIES. .ı. From Colum the territories used to be disciplined.

28. LET US HOPE GREAT DIGNITY, MANNA. .ı. Let us go to his trust, the great reverent one about heaven for us. Or, we hope great honour will be given to him on the head of these deeds. "Miad mair," that is, an abundance of "mann," that is, the *manna*. It is what the children of Israel used to say to their monks : "What is this but celestial food?" We hope therefore the great honour of the celestial food will be given to him.

29. CHRIST HAS ASSOCIATED HIM AMONG THE RIGHTEOUS. .ı. Christ will receive him into his association that is, into his familyship among the righteous, [that is] among angels and archangels.

30. THROUGH THE LONG PERIODS HE WAS HUMBLING HIMSELF. .ı. Through the long time he was at humbling here, that is, at devotion.

[CHAPTER VII.]

OF HIS PRUDENCE, AND READING, AND WISDOM.

1. A SAGE THE DOCTOR, WHO REACHED THE PATH OF FOUR. .ı. Sage is the doctor who reached the path of the four wisdoms.

2. COITLUIO La OOCETUL OO NIM·IaTh IaRN a CROICh. .ı. Iſ amlaıo oolluıo ſeom co ſaċ nıme ıaſn a cheſao ı ſoſ co cetul muıntıſe nıme ⁊ talman ; no ı tı[n]·ċlaıſ aıngel nıme.

3. CET CELL CUSTOIO TONO ſo oꝗı OIſſRINO. .ı. Rochoemeſtaſ cet cell ſo chomlaın-tıuſ tuınnı caılꝗ oſſſıno. No cet cell coſ a taet tono maſa : ⁊ cıntech aſ écıntec ano.

4. OLL NI' NI IOaL. .ı. Iſ oll ın tſen·ſeſ hé, ⁊ no con ıolaċt oozmt. No, oll anı oozmt oo maıch, ⁊ ní ıolaċt.
5. NI ELLASTAR CLOEN·ChLEIR. .ı. Nı aıleo na chaſa ınolıꝗteċa.
6. OO[S]ELLAR ſo INMUILC. .ı. Noſeꝗao eat ſo ınnıb an uılc : no, notaıoleo eat co taſſao a phennaıt cóıſ ſoſ cach. No, ba ꝗabaıl ella oo'no uaſul na cloen·ċhaſa, com bo maıth noımmuılꝗeo cſetım ſoſſu. No, noſblıꝗeo oo ſalluno .ı. oo oenam ſallaıno.

7. NI ſOE'T, NI ſUaCTNaO hERIS. .ı. Ní ſoſoıo nech uao oo oenam uılc, ⁊ nı ſoſʊ∵ċ[t]naıꝗ ſeın na heſıſ .ı. nı ſabı ſıſ comſaıſ[c]neċ aıcce ∴ heſeſ : no nı ſoaſlaıꝗ heſıſ ſoſ neċ.

8. NI aENEO NI' Na' buı IR RECT RI'ꝗ. .ı. Ní oénao ní oo aını act ıaſn [o]ıſꝗetaıo Oé .ı. naıneo ın oomnaıꝗıb. No, nı aıſoeſcaıꝗeo ní act oo ſeıſ ſíaꝗla Oé.

9. NaNO ETSa bas bITh .ı. aſ nao etao, no na bao ıſtao oo baſ tſıa bıchu, no ıſ ın bıch.

10. beo a aINM .ı. Iſoſ.
11. beo a aNUaIM .ı. a anım tall.
12. aO IMbUO ſOORUaIR ſo REChT NOEb .ı. Roſuſeſtaſ com beıth oo ſo oıſꝗetaıo na noeb. No, aſ a ſot ſooſubaſtaıſ ſo ſecht noeb—ıſ aıſ aſ beo a aınm ıſoſ: ⁊ a anım tall aſ ımmeo

2. HE WENT WITH MUSIC TO HEAVEN-LAND AFTER HIS CROSS. .i. It is how he went to the land of heaven after his suffering here, with the music of the family of heaven and of earth : or, in the chief-choir of the angels of heaven.

3. GUARDIAN OF A HUNDRED-CHURCHES UNDER FULL-NESS OF WAVES OF OFFERING. .i. He guarded a hundred churches under the completeness of the wave of the chalice of offering. Or, a hundred churches to which goes sea's wave ; and finite for indefinite in it.

4. A MIGHTY CHAMPION NOT BY AN IDOL. .i. He is a mighty champion, and not with idolism he works : or, mighty what he works of good, and not idolism.

5. HE BROUGHT NOT UP AN INIQUITOUS COMPANY. .i. He used not nourish the unrighteous companies.

6. HE BROUGHT THEM UP UNDER MILK. .i. He used to view them under the meanings of their evil : or, he used to try them that he might give his fit penance on each. Or, a catching of a flock for the noble one was the unjust companies, so that it might be well he would milk belief upon them. Or, he used to milk them for salt, that is, for the making of salt.

7. HE SUPPORTED NOT, HE ATTACKED NOT HERESY. .i. He sent not any from him for the doing of evil, and he attacked not himself any heresy ; that is, he had not an erroneous knowledge, that is, heresy. Or, he persuaded not heresy upon any one.

8. HE TOOK NO AMUSEMENT WHICH WAS NOT IN THE KING'S LAW. .i. He used to make nothing of amusement but according to God's law: that is, he used to take amuse-ment on Sundays. Or, he used to make nothing distin-guished but according to God's rule.

9. THAT HE MIGHT NOT GET ETERNAL DEATH. .i. That he might not get, or that there might not be destined for him death for ever, or in the world.

10. LIVING HIS NAME. .i. Here.

11. LIVING HIS SOUL. .i. His soul beyond.

12. IT IS A GREAT NUMBER THAT HE PREPARED UNDER SAINTS' LAW. .i. He procured that it (the number) might be for him under the law of the saints. Or, on account of the length of time he stayed under the law of the saints—

foopuaip .i. ap a pot : ap pit immeo [imoa ?] .i. pota,
ut oixit poeta :

> Ir imṫepc
> Cor int abcan oc imṫheċt :
> Int aboc o Rur ċaem Char,
> No con é a taeb ap imoa .i. pota.

13. **FRIShERT TINU A ṪOEh** .i. Ropiṫh bpúi
co ná p' bo ṫhiuċ a ṫóeb. " Fpirbept tinu a ṫhoeb " .i.
" pomaipneṛtap," ut oixit poeta :

> Neċ fpípbept a ṫijepna,
> Ni p'ba ile a líbepna,
> Cop pucait namait a cheno,
> A jabaip ir a oub-ceno

.i. a ech ocup a ċlaioeb: ap " colj " ocup " oub-ceno " ouo
nomina jlaoii punt ir int [p]en-Joeoilj, ut oixit poeta :

> Ni p' [b] fop bpaijtib oam na bo
> Fpométaip colj mo puanaoó:
> Fop bpaijtib pij foceipo feit
> Inoi Oub-ceno oc Oiapmait.

14. **TUIL A CUIRP CUILLSIUS** .i. Roċoilleptap
toill a ċuipp .i. ir e a milliuo a nemoenam.

15. **CUILL A NEOIT** .i. Rochuilleptap in jainni, ut
poeta oixit :

> In maith lib
> In tan apbepap fíp fpib ?
> Appaijep pepe paijit peoit :
> Ni jeib neoit fpi neċ ap oil

16. **NAO IN MACC MACC hUI ChUINO** .i.
Cuiċ in mac? Nin. em : mac hui Chuino .i. Colum Cille. No

it is on that account that his name is living here : and his
soul beyond on account of the number that he prepared
.ı. on account of its length : for " immed" means, namely,
" *long*," as the poet has said :

> Very thin is
> The dwarflet's leg a-walking—
> The dwarf from beautiful Ross Cas,
> By no means is it his side that is long. .ı. " fota."

13. DECAY ATTACKED HIS SIDE. .ı. Great running
of bowels until his side was not thick. " Frisbert tinu a
thoeb," that is, " romairnestar" (betrayed), as the poet has
said :

> One who betrayed his lord,
> His offspring were not numerous,
> Until enemies carried off his head,
> His " grey" and his " black-head."

That is, his *horse* and his *sword* : for " colg" and " dub-
cend" are two names for a *sword* in the old Goedilic, as the
poet has said :

> Not on throats of oxen or cows
> The sword of my hero is proven :
> On throats of kings it darts power—
> This same black-head with Diarmait.

14. THE DESIRE OF HIS BODY HE DESTROYED. .ı. He destroyed the desire of his body, that is, its destruction is its
non-performance.

15. HE DESTROYED HIS FIGHT. .ı. He destroyed the
power, as the poet said :

> Are ye pleased,
> When the truth is spoken to you ?
> Who follows love treasures follow ;
> He takes not fight against one who is dear.

15. IS NOT THE SON THE SON OF THE DESCENDANT OF
COND ? .ı. Whose is the son ? Not difficult indeed: the

H

ni bu in meic hui Chuino ʒainni, no neoci.   No, nao maicc
aonaċc maicc hui ċeo chuino .i. ni bui in maicc aċc báp
popḃċe .i. maicc hui cheo chuino ciċ .i. ni bui iapmua aċc
ba hua Cuino : quapi oixippec, " bá poep-ċlano cia popo-
oomaip món o Día."

17. **Cuil oeim oe eoc.** .i. Ní oepna oe eoc ní
nooíʒbao cuil .i. o'noí ap oemo .i. oiʒbaim.   No " oe póc"
ap choip ano .i. oe puachcain.

18. **Cuil oeim oe popmuc.** .i. Ní oepna oe
popmuc ní oiʒbap cuil.

19. **po lib liʒe, a ai, ap cech saeċ
sreca sina** .i. Ip maíċh lib, a eolchu, a liʒe
Coluim Cille, ap noícao a opuċc no a úp ap cachn
ʒalap, no[ṗ]paeċnaiʒeo paip na pina .i. cac pín a
[ṗ]pache.

20. **cria chuaich iolaiʒ oorumeoin
recu.** .i. lc oul oó cpía chuaiċ nan íoal popinnao am
biboanap ḟpi Oia, co cabpao poppu cpecim oo Oia:
⁊ o'noí ap "peacup" acá pécu.

21. **ar creola cairpciu.** .i. Ip aipe oopac
in mep-pa poppu ap in cappac cpeoal a cuipp ; no, ap a
cleipchechc popec a caippciu.

22. **cach si'r soich pir : piched pri
coluaim.** .i. Ropo puchain a chaċh ḟpi Oemon ⁊
Oomun, " poich píp" .i. popeċepcap pipinne : " piched ḟpi
culuain ;" .i. noṗúaċcnaiʒeo ḟpi á cholaino ipop.

23. **CO na reʒa in ri'ʒ-macc por
oe'oe oe'.** .i. No co paʒa mac in píʒ .i. Colum Cille,
pop ino apa epnail pil ic Oia.

son of the grandson of Cond, that is, Colum Cille. Or power or fighting was not the part of the son of the grand-son of Cond : or, was not the characteristic of the son who was buried that of the son of the grandson of Cond : that is, there belonged not to the son but a perfect death, that is, to the son of the grandson even of Cond indeed : that is, he was not a great grandson but he was a grandson of Cond. As if he had said, " he was a noble offspring, though he suffered much from God."

17. HE PROFANED NOUGHT ABOUT JEALOUSY. .ı. He did nothing about jealousy which would take away pro-fanity : from that which is "demo," that is, " I take away." Or, " de fot" is that which is right in it, that is, " about aggression."

18. HE PROFANED NOUGHT ABOUT ENVY. .ı. He did no-thing about envy which takes away profanity.

19. GOOD IN YOUR ESTIMATION (HIS) GRAVE, O SAGES, AGAINST EVERY SICKNESS OF COURSE OF SEASONS. .ı. "Good in your estimation, O learned, is the grave of Colum Cille," for its dew or its clay used to heal against every disease which the course of the seasons would extend, that is, every season its courses.

20. THROUGH AN IDOLATROUS TERRITORY HE MEDITATED CRIMINALITY. .ı. When going through the territory of the idols he would know their criminality towards God, so that he used to give on them belief in God: and from what is " reatus," *retu* is.

21. FOR THE SAKE OF RELIGIOUS CHARIOTS. .ı. It is why he gave this judgment on them for the religious chariot of their body : or, for his clericship he exchanged his chariots.

22. WITH CONTINUOUS BATTLE HE SOUGHT TRUTH: HE USED TO FIGHT AGAINST FLESH. .ı. His battle was con-tinual against Devil and World : " soich fir," that is, he sought truth : " fiched fri culuain :" he used to commit aggression against his flesh here.

23. THAT THE KING-SON MIGHT NOT COME ON THE SE-CONDARY OF GOD. .ı. By no means will the son of the king, that is, Colum Cille, come on the second division which is with God.

24. IN aChɜuCh, IN aChpeʀs. .ı. Ip ın
ɜuchn aıɜchıꝺe .ı. "Ice, maleꝺıccı:" no, "ın aɨɜuɨ" .ı. ıp
ın ɜuɨ pıl aıchle ɜocha aıle pemı. "In achpepp" .ı. nı ba
ıp ın pepp cánaıpe paɜap, acc ıp ın céc pepp .ı. "Uenıce,
beneꝺıccı, ⁊c."

25. aꝺʀaꝺNachC ʀıan a'es, ʀıan a
ımnıuʀC. .ı. ʀoaꝺnacc pıapıu cípaꝺ áep ꝺó .ı.
pıapıu pobo penoıp ⁊ pob' ampepcaɨ : ap ıc pé blıaꝺna
.lxx. pobo lán ꝺe.

26. aʀ ıppuʀNꝺ IN albu o'mun .ı. ap
omun ıppıpnꝺ ꝺochuaıꝺ ın albaın.
huc upque pexcum [capıculum.]

[capıculum uıı.]

IDEM DE COMMENDATIONE LAUDIS EIUS REGE NEPOTUM NEIL.

1. aeꝺ aCNoı ule oll-ꝺoıNe ꝺʀom-
cheCal. .ı. aeꝺ, mac aınmepech, ꝺopac .uıı. cumala
ꝺo'n ꝺull aıp aınm ꝺo chabaıpc ıp ın molaꝺ-pa choluım
chıllı : ⁊ poıaıɨnepcap aeꝺ ꝺo'n ꝺull commaꝺ ꝺpumıu
ceɨ cecal ın cecal-pa.
2. pechC apoʀ NIa Nem. .ı. In can popeɜaꝺ
ın cpen-pep .ı. Colum Cılle ; ap pıc nıa .ı. cpen-pep, uc
ꝺıcıcup :

> pıꝺcell Cpemchaınꝺ Nıaıꝺ Náıp
> Nıpbeıp mac bec ꝺo leıcáın:
> lech a poıpne ꝺ' óp buıꝺe,
> al leıɨ aıle ꝺ' [p]ınꝺpuıne.
> Oén-pep ꝺı a paıpınꝺ namma
> Noɨpenaꝺ pe ɨlánamna.

24. In second voice, in second verse. .i. In the fearful voice, namely, " Go ye cursed :" or, "in athguth," that is, in the voice which is after another voice before it. " In athfers," that is, it will not be in the second verse he will come, but in the first verse, that is, " Come, ye blessed, and so forth."

25. He was buried before age, before his weakness. .i. He was buried before his age came to him ; that is, before he was a senior, and was strengthless ; for it is six years [and] seventy that was full from it [the age].

26. On hell in Alba a terror. .i. For terror of hell he went to Alba.

Hither so far the sixth [chapter.]

[CHAPTER VII.]

OF THE COMMENDATION OF HIS PRAISE BY THE KING OF THE UI NEIL.

1. Aed laid down of all mighty-poems a poet-song. .i. Aed, son of Ainmere, who gave seven *cumals* for his name to be given in this praising of Colum Cille : and Aed laid down to the blind [Dallan] that more poetic than any song this song should be.

2. The time when the champion would reach heaven. .i. The time when the champion would come, that is, Colum Cille; for " nia" means, namely, a *champion*, as is said:

The chess-board of Cremthand Brave Champion—
A small child carries it not by little elbow:
Half of its party of yellow gold,
The other half of *findruine:*
One man of its party alone
Would purchase six couples.

3. NI ANDIL. .i. Ni p'bo nemoil la Dia hé, acc pobo
oil.

4. NI SUAIL. .i. Ní p[b'] bec hé. No, "ni hanoil" .i.
ni poinoil ┐ ní po[p]úaig ni ban puail.

5. NI SUAIG. .i. Ni popupuaig.

6. NI NIA NAO NUA PRI COTach
CONUAILL. .i. Ni cpén-pep nan nua inpó ppi cocac
.i. ppi glinniguo chocaig Conaill .i. ecep cuacha Conaill
apmeoon: no, ic oenam a cocaig ppi cuachaib ailib
oianechcaip. No, "ni nua" .i. no con[p]uil ocuno in cpen-
pep [p]uagep ní nua ppi cocac Conaill: ┐ "ní puaig"
copach na ceille píc. No, oan .i. ni pil ocuno in cpen-
pep achnuigep cocac Conaill: "ni nia" in copach pic.
"Ppi cocac Conuail" .i. ic píc ecep copp ┐ anmain.

7. CLUIOSIUS bORb beolu bennACht
bATAR IC TOI TOIL RIG. .i. Rocloi beolu innam
bopb bácap ic apo-píg Tói, cio eo bao aíl léo olc oo
páo, conio bennachao oogn'cip, uc puic balam.

8. O' DONIb DEIMTECTA, OC DEO DES-
SESTAR. .i. O' ooinib poóígbao, ic Dia cappapap.

9. AR AObUO, AR A'NI ATRONNAI AR-
GART GLAN hU'A hI CAThAIR CONUAIL. .i.
Ap a ainmni ┐ ap a áini poepnai gapcn glan hU'a
Conuaill inn a chacip. No, hua pom Coóíaip moip oo
Laignib il lech o machaip. No, ap aobchlop ocup ap
áini poepnai in gapc glan ┐c: ap ní oénao pom pein, uc
paciunc hipocpicae.

10. hIC UObUO CAIN·SRUITh SCEO MA-
GISTIR MUINTERE. "hic uobuo" .i. "nomen oolo-
pip" .i. ingiu pechi. Robo chain íapum in ppuich co na
coimleo magpe, co na pagbao in galap pein hé: ocup
oan pobo maigipcip muincepe imm on cécna. No, "ingu
pechi" .i. ip ipeccain pochogmaing a pechi hé ap immeo

3. NOT UNDEAR. .1. He was not undear with God, but he was dear.

4. NOT TRIFLING. .1. He was not small. Or, "ni handil," that is, he prepared not, and he knitted not anything which was trifling.

5. NOT PROSPEROUS. .1. He did not plan well.

6. THE CHAMPION IS NOT WHO BOUND NEW THINGS FOR THE ALLIANCE OF CONALL. .1. The champion of the new things is not here for alliance, that is, for confirming the alliance of Conall, that is, between the territories of Conall within; or, at making their alliance with other territories externally. Or, "ni nua" (a new thing), that is, there is not with us the champion, who will knit a new thing for the alliance of Conall; and "ni suaig," is the beginning of the sense thus. Or again, that is, there is not with us the champion who will renew the alliance of Conall: "ni nia" is the beginning thus. "Fri cotach Conuail," that is, at peace between body and soul.

7. HE SUBDUED WITH A BLESSING THE MOUTHS OF THE FIERCE WHO WERE AT TOY WITH KING'S WILL. .1. He subdued the mouths of the fierce, who were with the high king of Toi, though it was what they wished—to say evil, so that it is a blessing they used to make, as Balam was.

8. FROM MEN WITHDRAWN WITH GOD HE HAS TAKEN HIS SEAT. .1. From men he was taken away; with God he has rested.

9. FOR ABSTEMIOUSNESS, FOR FASTING, THE DESCENDANT BESTOWED PURE GREAT HOSPITALITY IN [THE] CITY OF CONALL. .1. On account of his abstemiousness, and on account of his fasting, the descendant of Conall distributed pure hospitality in his city. Or, a descendant of Cathair Mor was he in the side from mother. Or, for pleasure and for amusement he distributed the pure hospitality, and so forth: for he used not to do that, as the hypocrites do.

10. AT DECIDING A FAIR SENIOR AND A MASTER OF FAMILY. .1. "Hic udbud," that is, a name of a disease, that is, "tightness of skin." The senior was accordingly fair, so that he used not to eat fish lest that disease should seize him: and likewise he was master of a family about the same matter. Or, "tightness of skin," that is, it is hardly his skin surrounded him on account of the abund-

a ban; no "ic uobuo" .1. ic pethuguo aobb ic éipniuo
chept na canoni : No "ic uobuo" .1. ic bibouo [na]n̂ goa :
no, "ic uobuo" .1. ic poibaouo .1. ic bavuo cuipp Cpipt
po a [p]uil ic oppmiuno : no, aínm oo boith légíno, no
ppoppii loci 1 Ceneol Chonaill.

11. PRI ANZEL NACALLASTAR : ATZAILL
ZRAMMATAIZ ZREIC .1. Oognio aingel o'accal-
laim, ocup popoglainn gpammataig amal Zpecu. No,
noaicilleo gpammatacou ocup Zpécu.*

12. SOER SECH TUAICH SIN hINEOIM .1.
Saep nopechtep pecht tuatha, ꞇ cinntech ap écinnteċ
ano, nó coic tuaċa Epeno ꞇ oi thuaich in Albain. No,
nopechtea pectap-ċuaich : no, ba paep nopechtaip
pipinoe ip in cip thuaio. "Sin inecum" .1. ip amlaio pin
oognio a paipneip, ap pic pin .1. amlaio, ut oixit poeta :

Ipín teit in mal 'm a ċech pig,
In oegiult cen cappaip cpit,
Con ouib-ciuno in a oag-pcip.

.1. cip (.1. lam) onoí ap "capio."

13. MAC PEOLIMIO[E] PICH TUAICH PINN
OUT. .1. Mac Peolimio[e] oia pichtip, no oia pognatip
in pice tuach : ꞇ cinotech ap ecinntech ann beop : no,
oi a pich in cip ċuaig. "Pinn ouit" .1. pinem munoi ; no,
popitip cpich ꞇ comlainep in popcetail, no a bap pén.
No, pín ineoim mac Peolimio[e]. Pino .1. ip é inoipim
amlaio pin mac Pioilmio[e] ap in pich atuaig.

14. NI TOICHES OO'N BITH BA SIR OO
CHROICHE CUMNI .1. Ní ma túoċaio pop bith che
ap gaipoe a ampipe : pobo cputhain oo ċuimniugo
cpoiche pop a ċopp. No, ní can ċéppao oocuaio oo'n
bith oo lucht Toi : no, ni pobo toi oo lucht in betha in

---

* With this word ends imperfectly the copy in Lebor na hUidre : the remainder
is from Lebor Brecc.—[ED.]

ance of his qualifications : or, "ic udbud," that is, at the perceiving of difficulties in explaining the questions of the Canon. Or, "ic udbud," that is, at destroying the false-hoods : or, "ic udbud," that is, at submerging, that is, at dipping the body of Christ under his blood at Mass : or, it is a name for a reading hut, or of a special place in Cenel Chónaill.

11. To AN ANGEL HE USED TO SPEAK : HE SPOKE GREEK GRAMMAR. .ı. He used to address an angel, and he learned grammar like Greeks. Or, he used to address grammarians and Greeks.

12. A NOBLE ONE WHO SOUGHT NORTH : THIS ONE I RE-LATE. .ı. A noble one who sought seven territories, and de-finite for indefinite in it, or, the five territories of Eriu, and two territories in Alba. Or, he used to seek extern territory: or, it was noble he followed truth in the north territory. " Sin inetum," .ı. it is thus he makes its narra-tion, for " sin" means, namely, *thus*, as the poet said :

In this manner the chief goes round his house of a king,
In good raiment without a storm-shower through it,
With his black head (sword) in his good grip (in his right hand).

That is, " cip," (hand) from the word *capio* (I hold).

13. FEDILMID'S SON IN THE NORTH TERRITORY KNEW END· .ı. The son of Fedilmid for whom used to fight, or whom used to serve the twenty territories: and definite for inde-finite in it still : or from whom the north country boiled. " Finn ouit," that is, the end of the world : or he knew the end and completeness of the doctrine, or his own death. Or, thus I relate the son of Fedilmid. " Find": that is, it is he I relate thus—the son of Fedilmid from the territory in the north.

14. THERE WENT NOT FROM THE WORLD [ONE] WHO WAS MORE CONTINUAL FOR CROSS'S REMEMBRANCE. .ı. Not well he came on this world on account of the shortness of his time : he was everlasting for the remembering of a cross on his body. Or, not without suffering he went from the world for the people of Tay: or, there was not silence for the people of the world, when he suffered. Or, there came

can pocheraip pium.　No, ni canic do'n bich hille bid
puchaine do cuimniugud cnochi Cpipc.

15. CONFIZ FIZLESCAR O ZNIM ZLIN-
DESCAR. .i. Inní nofized, no nofuaided, no nofezad
o fizill impaice do denam, no nozlindead o znim: no,
nozlindiz o znim quod ppedicapec uepbo, uc dicicup:
"Implewic faccip quod ppedicauic uepbip:" ⁊ dan
copezad fizill do denam .i. da cec deac plechcain.

16. CONZEIN DE ZEINN AN hua aiRC,
NIS NEILL CO NERC. .i. Co pozein de pin co p'ba
zein opdnize he.　No, pozenaip zeinn an de .i. hua
Aipc mic Cuind eride, no hua Neill.　No, zein fin
pozenip de: zein eipdaipc, pacmap, "Concepc" [recte
co nepc] .i. pobo nepcmap.　No, "nipneill co nipc" .i.
ni fpi nepcaib claimni Neill dobepead coeb, acc fpia
nepcu in Spipuca noeib.　No pic: "hua Aipc nip Neill
co nipc" .i. ni a nipc Aipc no Neill nobazad, cia p'ba
paep-chlano.

17. NAC FuICh FeChC DI am baChaR.
.i.　Ni depna puachcain in bud chóip a bap di am
bad he fein nobeci do chena: no, ni depna puachcain
fechc acbach .i. ni oc mapbad neich ele acbach.

18. buICh bRON CERD CUIND DUL DO
DRuib MeCi maICh. .i.　Robpip bpon-cach fop
Chono .i. Lech Cuind con a eladain ap dul do Col.
Cilli do chaippin uaidib: no, pobui uch ⁊ bpon hi
ceind Chuind .i. in eladain, no in écpi Chuind: no
pobui bpipped ⁊ bpon hi cacaip Chuind do'n dpuib
pobi fop Colum Cilli dian dechaid anund: no, do'n
bpon ⁊ coippe canic hil Leich Cuind iapn éc Coluim
Cilli.　"Meci maich" .i. ip mop meic in machiupa
bui do a cpuib bui faip.

19. maC-aINm CRuIChe. .i.　Dopac ainm do
chpoich: no mac pip bud chumain ainmin chpoiche
Cpipc: no, ip aip-ainim chpóm duind in mac pochep and.

not to the world hither [one] who was more everlasting for
the remembering of the cross of Christ.

15. THE CONWEB HE FIGULATED FROM DEED HE FOL-
LOWED .ı. The thing he used to weave, or he used to sow, or
he used to view from figulation, he used to meditate to do,
or he used to follow from deed: or, he illustrated from deed
what he would preach in word ; as is said : "he fulfilled in
deeds what he preached in words," and also he used to view
to make figulation, that is, twelve thousand prostrations.

16. SO THAT THERE SPRUNG FROM IT A NOBLE OFFSPRING,
A DESCENDANT OF ART, NOT OF NIALL WITH STRENGTH. .ı.
So that there sprung from that that he was an illustrious
offspring.   Or, an illustrious offspring was born from it, that
is, a descendant of Art, son of Cond, was he ; or a descendant
of Niall.   Or, a true offspring was born from it ; an offspring celebrated, full of grace.   " Concert [*recte*, co nert],
that is, he was strong.   Or, " nis Neill co nirt," that is,
not with the powers of the *Clanna* Neill he used to side,
but with the powers of the Holy Spirit.   Or, thus: " Hua
Airt nis Neill co neirt" .ı. not from the power of Art or of
Niall he used to boast, though he was a noble offspring.

17. WHO COMMITTED NOT AN INJURY FOR WHICH ONE
DIES. .ı. He committed not an injury for which his death
would be just, if it were itself that were for him already :
or, he committed not an injury when he was dying, that is,
it is not at killing another one he died.

18. THE PROFESSION OF COND BROKE GRIEF THROUGH HIS
GOING FOR A STAY OF GREATNESS OF GOOD. .ı. There broke a
grief-battle on Cond, that is, Cond's Half, with its science
on Colum Cille's going for a stay from them: or, there
were wail and grief in the profession of Cond, that is, in the
science, or in the poetry of Cond: or, there were misery
and grief in the city of Cond from the stay which was on
Colum Cille when he went over ; or, from the grief and
sadness which came into Cond's Half after the death of
Colum Cille.   "Meti maith," that is, large is the greatness
of the goodness which was to him from the stay which
was on him.

19. A SON-NAME OF CROSS. .ı. He gave name to a cross :
or, a son to whom was mindful the name of Christ's cross :
or, a heavy back-blemish to us is the son who suffered in it.

20. CUICE aias: ECE aeR: CERCO INOIaS
.ı. Conıce ro a aer con eɲbaılꞇ. "Ece" .ı. "ıɼ ꝼolluɼ
ꝺam ınꞇ aeɲ hı ceın aꞇu oc ꝺenam huıuɼ lauoıɼ:" aɲ
ꝺolecꞇhea ꝺo a ɼuıle ceın buı oc ꝺenam ın molꞇa.
"Cеɲꞇo ınꝺıaɼ" .ı. ıɼ moɲ a cheɲꞇı ınꝺıɼımm, no
ceɲꞇaıꝺe ınꝺıɼım.

21. alliach leo binꝺ hı [S]NECCO NU-
Oal. .ı. alliach .ı. al-lıch ıꝺem ocuɼ lích a aılle : amaıl
ɡláeıꝺ leomaın bınꝺ hı ɼnechꞇa ın ꞇáıl nuı aılle ınꝺ leıch
.ı. Colum Cılle : aɲ ın ꞇan ꝺoɼbeɲeaꝺ ın leo a ɡlaeıꝺ
aɼɼ, ꞇecaıꞇ na hulı anmunna ꝼuꞇhı co ꞇabaıɲ ꞇíí ꝺı
a eɲbul ımmpo, con eplеꞇ ıɼ ın luc ɼın ɼeꝺ luch ⁊
ɼınꝺach. Cıc ın ɼelche chuıce-ɼıum ıaɲ ɼın co ꞇábaıɼ
ɼenıꞇe ımme-ɼıum poɼꞇ con epıl. Sıc Colum Cılle.
Inꞇíí ım a ꞇabꝺaꝺ ꞇíí a ɼoɲcеꞇaıl, nı ꞇheıɡеꝺ uaꝺ:
ꞇaıɼɼe ɼеꝺ anꝺɼecꞇaıꝺ ꞇíí ɼoɲcеꞇaıl Mıc Oe ın a
chımcell ɼom. No, "all-ıaꞇh" .ı. hın ıaꞇh hı nalla, aɲ
ꞇеıꞇ ın leo ın ıaꞇh ın alla ceın bıɼ ın coıɼne, co ꞇabaıɲ a
ɡlaeıꝺ aɼɼ ıaɲn ꝺul hı mach ıɼ ın ꝺaıl nuı. hınꝺ aılle
ꝺon ꝺoɡnıꝺ Col. Cılle co ꝺuɼcaꝺ na manach hım
ıaɲmeɲɡı ɼoɲaıchmenꞇaɼ hıc. No "allhıaꞇh" .ı. aɲoıle
anmunna ⁊ ꞇɲı ꝼaꞇɼıne occa .ı. ɼɼеɼеnɼ ⁊ ɼɼеꞇеɲıcum
⁊ ꝼuꞇuɼum, con ınꝺꞇɼamlaıcheɲ Colum Cılle ꝺo ɼın,
aɲ ɼobaꞇaɼ na ꞇɼеꝺe ɼın occa. No, "bınꝺ ꝺo neoch
ꝺo nu-ꝺál" .ı. ıɼ bınꝺ ı ɼеcꞇ-ɼa hı nú-ꝺál .ı. ın ꝺál nua
.ı. aınɡıl ɼucɼaꞇ leo ın leo ıɼ ın all-ıaꞇh ınnꞇɼamlaıɡꞇech
.ı. ın coelum.

22. CO EC CO ECUaIS INCECh hı CO-
luaIN CO hECheR : a ROɡU ROꝼER suba
SaM-SICh. .ı. Co m' ec no con ınꝺıɼıub ɼcela Coluım
Cıllı: no quanꝺo, uꞇ ꝺıcıꞇuɼ "co amm" .ı. c' ınꝺuɼ ınꝺıɼɼеꞇ
co m' ec ɼcela Coluım Cıllı, aɲ ní ꞇalla ꝼoɲm-ɼa an
ınꝺuɼ [ɼ]ın .ı. ınꞇech ꝺocuaıꝺ hı colaınꝺ co heꞇheɲ, amaıl
ꝺochuaıꝺ Pol : ocuɼ ba he a ɲoɡa ɼın, aɲ ꞇeıɡeꝺ cec
ꝺaɲꝺaın ceın buı hı colaınꝺ aꝺ coelum, uꞇ ꝼeɲunꞇ ɼeɲıꞇı.
"Roꝼеɲ" .ı. ɼoꝼeɲuɼꞇaɲ a ɲoɡa cuɼ ın ɼıch hı ꝼıl ɼıch ⁊
ɼuba : no, ɼoꝼeɲuɼꞇaɲ co ꞇaɲꝺaꝺ a ɲoɡu ꝺo co ɼam-

20. HITHERTO AGE: MANIFEST SKY : PROFESSIONS I HAVE
RELATED. .ı. Up to this his age until he died. "Ece," that
is, "manifest to me the sky while I am at making of this
praise:" for his eyes were allowed to him while he was at
making of the praise. "Certo indias," that is, "great his
professions I relate," or, "truthful I relate."

21. HE CRIED A MELODIOUS LION IN A SNOW'S NEW
MEETING. .ı. "Alliath," that is, "al-lith," the same as
"lith a aille" (the vigour of his praise) : like the roar of a
melodious lion in snow in a new meeting is the praise of the
strong one, that is, Colum Cille: for when the lion gives
his roar out of him all the animals come at it, until he
gives a coil of his tail around them, so that there die in
that place a flock of rats and of foxes. The hunter comes
to him then until he gives nets about him afterwards,
so that he dies. Thus Colum Cille. The person around
whom he would give the coil of his teaching would not
go from him : the strong power of the coil of the instruction of the Son of God remains around him. Or, "alliath," that is, "hin iath in alla" (in the land of the cave),
for the lion goes to the land of the cave, while the frost
remains, so that he gives his roar out of him after going
out into the new meeting. The praise, then, which Colum
Cille makes for the awakening of the monks about midnight,
is commemorated here. Or, "Allhiath," that is, a certain
animal and three prophecies with it, namely, the present
and past and the future: so that Colum Cille is likened to
this one, for he had these three. Or, "bind do neuch do
nu-dal," that is, he is melodious this time "hi nu-dal," that
is, in a new meeting, that is, angels that carried with
them the lion into the comparative cave-land, that is, into
heaven.

22. UNTIL DEATH HOW SHALL I RELATE A ROUTE IN
FLESH TO HEAVEN? HIS CHOICE MADE A JOY CALM-
PEACE. .ı. Until my death I shall not by any means relate the tidings of Col. Cille, or *when*, as is said, "co
amm" (what time?) that is, in what manner shall I
relate until my death the tidings of Colum Cille, for that
manner fits not on me : that is, a route he went in flesh to
heaven, as Paul went : and that was his choice, for he
used to go every Thursday while he was in flesh to heaven,
as the learned say. "Rofer," that is, he effected his

ric .i. co rich inc rampaio, an ir ano acbach. No, ropuip rich oi a cramao in techc oóchoio hin echep.

23. ROSOLUI SOCHLA SUIDE DODERB. .i.
Ropuaplaic puiche . . . . . . "Depb" .i. ir demin dopigne rin.

24. NI ONG OEN-TIGE, NI ONG OEN-TETI.
.i. Ong .i. uch .i. ni huch oen-cige .i. ni an oen-cig aca a chainiuo, reo in mulcip oomibur. Sic in requence. No "ong" .i. caoall: no ceo .i. ciminpain, no ceo .i. plige : ni caoall oen-cige iapoin, no ni caoall oen ceci, no caoall oen-pligeo ounn coineo Coluim Cilli. Ubi erc ong .i. caoall .nin. hi Pocha bpech, uc oicicup : "Ongaib, corcaib capuc" .i. an óman a caoaill oi a corc oia caipoib. "Ong" .i. ongain : Ni p'bo hongain oen-cige, reo, nob ongain ill-cige : no, ni p'bo hongain oen-pligeo, reo mulcapum.

25. CROM-TUATH POCUL POTHUIND. .i.
Ir cpomm cuach, no ir cpóm a chaineo oc na cuachaib, 7 pocul gonap nech pocuino. No, "pocul pochuino" .i. pocheino cach uch : no poceno .i. pocul porenoap cach in pcel-pa.

26. ARDLECHT DE LOCHARN IN RIG DORADBUD ROATHLAS. .i.
Ir apo-pollur como lochapn. No "in lochapn in pig," oe poolechcc oino in molao-pa pop Colum Cille in pegno coelopum. Uel ric : cia poóibao hibupp poáclapp call. "Roolechc oo lochapn in pig" .i. Colum "cia pobaioeo hic co poachlap call," 7 pic concigic ei.

27. AMRAD INSO IN RIG RODOMRIG—PORDONSNAIDPE SIONE. .i.
Ir ampa in pao ro, no ampa in pach : no ampeio (.i. oooaing). No ampa in

choice to the palace in which are peace and joy : or, he effected that his choice was given to him until summer-peace, that is, to the peace of the summer, for it is in it he died. Or, the surety who went to heaven prepared peace for his congregation.

23. THE GOOD MAN RESOLVED UNCERTAIN WISDOM. .ı. He resolved wisdom ...... to them. "Derb," that is, it is certain he did that.

24. NOT THE WAIL OF ONE HOUSE, NOT THE WAIL OF ONE STRING. .ı. "Ong," that is, "uch," that is, not the wail of one house, that is, not in one house is the wailing of him, but in many houses : so in the following. Or "ong," that is, *tribulation;* or, "ted," that is a *tympanum,* or "ted," that is, *way :* not the tribulation of one house then, nor the tribulation of one tympanum, nor the tribulation of one road for us, is crying Col. Cille. Where is "ong," that is, *tribulation?* Not difficult: in Fotha Breth, as is said : "Ongaib, coscaib carut" (with tribulations, corrections of friends), that is, for fear of their tribulation from the correcting of them by their friends. "Ong," that is, "ongain," (....) : it was not an "ongain" of one house, but of many houses : or, it was not an "ongain" of one way, but of many.

25. OF HEAVY TERRITORIES IS A WORD OF NOISE. .ı. The territory is heavy, or heavy is the crying for him with the territories, and a word which wounds one is "fothuind." Or, "focul fothuind," that is, soreish is every wail, or "fothend," that is, a word which presses every one is this news.

26. IT WAS DUE TO THE LAMP OF THE KING WHICH WAS EXTINGUISHED, THAT IT RELIGHTED. .ı. He is high-bright, so that he is a lamp. Or, "the lamp of the king," from it was due to us this praising on Col. Cille in the kingdom of heaven. Or thus : though it was extinguished here, it relighted beyond. "It was due to the lamp of the king," that is, Colum, "though it was extinguished here, that it relighted beyond" ; and thus it happened to him.

27. THIS IS THE ELEGY OF THE KING, WHO HAS KINGED ME—MAY IT CONDUCT US TO SION. .ı. Wonderful is this saying, or wonderful the grace : or, "amreid," that is,

puc nan ala fil foi in uarrana. No ir inano inc "am"
fil ano ⁊ "morr" ar port mortem precium lauoir
oacum ert coeco: ar ir inano inc "am" ⁊ "nem" .i.
nem-pach oin, ar ir neam chucao oo hil log a molta in
pig. "Rocampig-ra" .i. oopat pige oam-ra, ar ir ee Colum Cille oopat ollamnar oam. "Fornonrnaioe Sione"
.i. prnaioe co Sliab Sion .i. cur in cathpaig nemoai.

28. ROCOMSIB-SA SECH RIAGU. .i. "Roria

rinoe chuca rech in luchc bite oc piagao caich." .i.
oemna: "no pomuca rech oemna in aeoir ao pequiem
ranccorum." No "rech piagu" .i. rech ingene Oircc:
trer filiae horcci quae oiuerrir nominibur nominancur
in coelo ⁊ in terra ⁊ inferno. In coelo quioem Sthenio
⁊ Euriale [⁊] Meoura: in terra Clotho, Lacherir,
Atropor: in inferno Alecto, Megaera, Teriphone.

29. RORElO MENMA OUBA OlM. .i. "Robo

ropaio oam oul rech na oemna ouba" .i. ubi runt
oemoner: ⁊ mentitum .i. go, mentita .i. goa .i. Robo
peio namra oul rech na goa ouba: no, poerpeoi oimm
oemna ouba: no, pob' aporaio oo na lochtai, no na goa
ouba hi menmain oo chor oimm. No, penigrio ⁊ lafio
oimm na breca ouba liferr Oemun form."

30. OOMCIFE CEN AINME HUA CUIRP[RI] CATHRA CON UAISLE

.i. "Conab capa
oam cen ainim hoa oo Choirpri Nia-per oo Laignib:"
ar ir hii Ethni, ingen Oimma meic Noe, a mathair, oo
Choirprige Laigen, ut oicitur:

> Ethni airechoa 'n a biu,
> In rigan oo Chorprigiu,
> Mathair Choluim, comalln gle,
> Ingen Oimmai, meic Noe.

Ocur baba hua hinn Noe rin oo Chathair Mor, mac

difficult. Or, wonderful the course of the Alas (Alleluias) that follow the Hosanna. Or, the "am" that is in it is the same as "death," for after death the reward of the praise was given to the Blind (Dallan): for the "am" is the same as "nem" (heaven), that is, heaven-reward, for it is heaven that was given to him in price of the praising of the king. "Rotamrigsa," that is, "who gave sovereignty to me, for it is Colum Cille who gave *Ollamnas* (office of chief poet) to me." "Fordonsnaide Sione," that is, may he conduct us to Mount Sion, that is, to the heavenly city.

28. .1. MAY HE BRING ME PAST TORMENTS. .1. "May he bring us to him past the crew, who are tormenting every one," that is, demons: or, "may he waft me past the demons of the air to the peace of the saints." Or, "sech riagu," that is, past the daughters of Phorcus: these are three daughters who are named with different names in heaven, in earth, and in hell. In heaven, indeed, Sthenyo, and Euryale [and] Medusa: in earth Clotho, Lachesis, Atropos: in hell, Alecto, Megaera, Tesiphone.

29. MAY HE DRIVE MIND-GLOOM FROM ME. .1. "May it be easy for me to go past the black demons," that is, where demons are: and "mentitum," that is, *a lie*, and "mentita," that is, *lies*. That is, "May it be easy for me to go past the black lies; or, may he expel off me black demons: or, may it be easy for him to put off me the faults, or the black lies in my mind. He will loose and put off me the black lies which the demon will pour on me."

30. MAY THE DESCENDANT OF CORPRE OF THE CITY WITH NOBILITY SEE ME WITHOUT STAINS. .1. "May the descendant of Coirpre Niafer of the Laigne be a friend to me without stain": for Ethne, daughter of Dimma, son of Noe, is his mother, of the Coirprige of the Laigne, as is said:

> Ethne principal when alive,
> The queen of the Corprigi; ·
> Mother of Colum—a clear fulfilment—
> Daughter of Dimma, son of Noe.

And that Noe was a descendant of Cathair Mor, son of

Feolimio Fir-unglari, "Con uar[li]" .i. hua Chachaip
uarail in Coirppe rin.

31. OLL-Racha ROoiall, oll - Nacha
Nime NemoRian Ni oam uain. Ni oi[s]
sceoil oo hua Neill .i. Ir mor in rooiall
.i. in rogneiuguo ⁊ in cruchuguo ⁊ in oiol ooracur forr
na foclu-ra anuarr. "Oll-nacha" .i. molao : no, ir
uille na inoar cac nach oorigneo oo nim ⁊ oo gnein hin
nime in nach-ro. No, ir oll in nach oognicir na filio
for cur oo gnein ⁊ oo erca, ⁊ ní moo in oeimniugao
oobertir forrai olcar ooracur-[r]a runo: no, cio oll
lino enoancur nacha gneine ⁊ erca, ni moo lino, ol in
file, olcar ennoancur ecrechca Choluim Cilli. "Ni oam
uain" .i. ar coecacur erc icerum .i. ni huain oam .i. "ni
[f] ecaim in molao oo oenam rech aro, ar ruccha mo
ruile uaimm." No sic: "ni oam uain fri a oenam hin
nacha cu holl, ar niraicim nem na gnein. "Ni oi[r]
rceoil" .i. ni can rcel oo huib Neill rin anuarr.

FIN. IT. AMEN.

REMARKS ON TEXT, &c.

THERE are a few complete copies of the "Amra," besides
that of Lebor na hUidre, which is the oldest and the best :
in Part II. I shall occasionally refer to those copies.

Except in the Introduction I had intended to write the
English form "Colum" invariably, as it is the most usual
in the Amra, but I find that in some places *Columb* has
found its way into the translation : the oldest Irish form is
Colomb.

In representing the original I have made no distinc-
tion between uncontracted and contracted syllables, as
I could not do so without disfiguring the page with
the introduction of either Roman characters, or brackets,

Fedelmid Fir-urglas. "Con uais[le]," .i. a descendant of noble Cathair is that Coirpre.

31. GREAT CIRCLES OF GREAT TURNINGS, GREAT POEMS OF HEAVEN TO ME SUNLESS IS NOT A SUITABLENESS. NOT A TRIFLE OF A STORY ABOUT UA NEILL. .i. Great is the great declension, that is, the great formation and the shaping, and the finish I have given on these words. above. "Oll-natha," that is, praising: or, greater than every poem which has been made for heaven and for the sun of the heaven is this poem. Or, great is the poem the poets used to make at the beginning for the sun and moon, and not greater the confirmation they used to give on it than I have given here: or, though great in our estimation is the celebrity of the poems of the sun and moon, not greater in our estimation, says the poet, than the celebrity of the death of Col. Cille. "Nidamuain," that is, for I am blinded again, that is, "ni huain dam" (there is no opportunity for me), that is, I cannot make the praise beyond this, for my eyes have been taken from me. Or, thus: I have no opportunity of making the poem mightily, for I see neither heaven nor sun. "Ni dis [s]ceoil," that is, not without a story for the descendants of Niall that down.

IT ENDETH. AMEN.

---

or something in that way, to indicate the resolution of the contraction. Meantime, while I have thus preserved a uniformity pleasing to the eye, I have done no injustice to the student, for in the accurate lithograph copy of Leb. na hUidre, published some time ago by the Royal Irish Academy, he can see the contraction at a glance, while from the present edition he can test my mode of resolving it.

As I had no opportunity of representing in print the dotted n and m, I shall here point out the words in which they occur :

The n of ruiln, p. 8, line 17 : the m of ceopam, and of bliavanm, p. 10, fourth line from foot : the n of cing, next line : the second n of cenonaib, p. 14, line 1: the n of vopaippngepc, same page, line 2 : the second n of nongeban, ib., line 4 : the n of ın in laṗ ın ᵹóevel, ib., seventh line from foot : the n of ın and ᵹucn, ib., sixth and fifth line from foot, and p. 16, line 13 : the n of veilmn and vı[ṗ]olaınᵹ, p. 24, Article 1, and again, Article 3: the m of aınm bıu, p. 28, Article 9 : the n of anᵹıl Oé, p. 30, Article 1 : the n of anᵹıl, p. 32, Article 13 : the n of v'anᵹıl, p. 38, Article 9 : the n of ımmevn, p. 40, Article 11 : the n of anᵹel, p. 64, Article 11.

Corrections of text.—ınv ınnaṗba, p. 8, line 10 [*ms.* ın cınnaṗba]: ṗuc, p. 12, line 9 from foot [*ms.* ṗuċ]: ṗcíṫ, p. 16, line 12 [*ms.* ṗcív] : ı cṗúb, p. 18, line 15 [*ms.* íċṗub]: veṗmeṗeċcaıᵹcıṗ, p. 18, line 8 from foot [*ms.* veṗ—] vocuıṗınec p. 20, line 3 [*ms.* vocuıṗmec] : ṗenċaıv, p. 24, Article 3 [*ms.* ṗeṗċaıv]: ṗlunev, p. 28, Article 13 [*ms.* ṗlunenv, with the second n dotted to indicate *deletion*]: vınv, p. 32, Article 7 [*ms.* bınv]: 'n a cṗıvıb, p. 32, Article 11 [*ms.* naċṗıvıb]: aınᵹıl Oé, p. 32, Article 13 [*ms.* aınᵹel Oé] : nochlunev p. 36, Article 3 [*ms.* nochlunev]: ınc éc, p. 38, Article 8 [*ms.* ıncéċ]: voṗcanav, p. 40, Article 11 [*ms.* voṗcaṗav]: nı nıa, p. 62, line 6 [*ms.* nıma].

Translation: For comma after " north-west," p. 11, fifth line from foot, read "period:" for " treasures," p. 13, line 11, read " gifts:" for twenty-fifth line, p. 13, read " O conscience with its soul pure :" to " Obscuration," p. 17, seventh line from foot, prefix " Culu," that is : " for " wander" p. 27, line 15, read " dwell:" p. 43, Article 7, dele *comma* after " Maistin :" for " finite, p. 55, Article 3, read " definite." In the translation there are, no doubt, some contestable and absolutely erroneous renderings: these, however, I must leave in the care of my readers until I examine them in the Second Part.

I find *one* error in the printed Irish—ınvbaıv [recte ınbaıv] p. 16, line 18. For lıbuṗ-leıᵹvocc, p. 32, Article 7, read lıbuṗ leıᵹ vocc : *dele* hyphen in ṗoleṗ-aıl, same page, Article 9.

N.B.—The " Amra," which in the original is written in double column each page, begins at top of p. 5, and breaks up at foot of p. 12. The supplement from the Leb. Brecc is from the back of fol. 110.